Retirement Money Wave

Generate Automatic Tax-Free Income for the Rest of Your Life

Steve Burton

www.retirementmoneywave.com

Books are available for special promotions and premiums. For details, contact Special Markets, LINX, Corp., Box 613, Great Falls, VA 22066, or e-mail specialmarkets@linxcorp.com.

ISBW-13: 978-9369610-0-9
ISBW-10: 1936961008

Book design by Paul Fitzgerald
Editing by Sandra Gurvis

Published by LINX

LINX, Corp.
Box 613
Great Falls, VA 22066
www.linxcorp.com

Printed in the United States of America

Dedication

*Personally I want to thank God for all that
I have and also my dear wife of over 30 years,
Annette, my two sons, Kevin and Adam,
my parents Wayne and Pat Burton and all
of my mentors over the years, whose time and
hard work helped me be where I am today.
I want to also mention my late grandfather
Marl Burton, whose caring nature was
instrumental in developing my love of business.*

*And lastly to the hardworking American
taxpayers struggling to maintain a lifestyle and
raise their children and who hopefully have some
golden years to look forward to.*

Disclaimer

The equity indexed universal life insurances (EIULs) discussed in this book are not investments - they are insurance policies that have accumulation accounts linked to a financial index. Their performance varies based on the product used, method of funding, size of the policy and performance of the index. All life insurance policies have sales charges, maintenance fees and the cost of insurance. Last but certainly not least, EIULs should be reviewed with a competent and licensed financial services professional before they are purchased.

Contents

Funding Your Personal Pension Plan

Create Your Legacy

Summary – Some "Final" Answers

Introduction - Read This First!

Creating Your Personal Retirement Money Wave

The development of the Retirement Money Wave strategy came about through a circuitous route. Having been a business owner for over 30 years, I have made a lot of decisions. Many were by trial and error and frankly, some were not very smart. And when mistakes did occur, it was because I reacted based on emotion, rather than common sense.

Steve Burton: Catching the Wave

My first business – which I started in 1979 and still own – was a commercial cleaning company. One weekend I helped out some friends and before I knew it, I had my own enterprise. The first few years were difficult; we'd win contracts, only to lose them again; while at other times, we made money. It wasn't until 1988 that I found a mentor with his own large cleaning business to teach me what he knew. I became a subcontractor for him, and within months my own business grew dramatically and has provided a substantial income for my family and myself ever since.

Even though I'd been doing many things correctly before, my mentor helped me refine and tweak certain aspects that helped grow my business dramatically, thus providing the basis for my own financial security. If a district or regional manager called with a problem, we would go see them in person, to make sure it got taken care of. It was our job to make sure that the clients – who were busy with their own lives and responsibilities – had one less thing to worry about. My mentor told me that if a manager called with a problem, we needed to make sure it was fixed within 24 hours. These minor adjustments, many of which are just plain old common sense, helped me grow my business.

The same basic rules apply to the financial services business. If you provide a solution to people's problems and concerns, and put their money to work for them without risk, they will be clients for life.

I wish I'd sought help sooner, although maybe learning the hard way allowed me to better implement the tools and ideas more successfully. Hopefully you'll be as receptive to the suggestions and ideas in this book. Mentors have helped me create at least two very profitable businesses, and my hope is that we can mentor you to find your path to financial freedom.

While the cleaning business was not my first choice of a vocation, it was something I knew, and it has provided a wonderful lifestyle for my family. Additionally, I loved making money and discovered I liked helping others do the same. When I ventured into the financial services business in the late 1990s, I knew I had found my calling. I could make a great income by helping others profit and grow their wealth! I personally believe this is why I was put on this earth.

Again, though, I struggled for years looking for a niche market that would offer something unique to clients. Even back then, it was obvious to me that traditional retirement and savings strategies were ineffective. Few Americans were achieving wealth, with only about 3 percent of the population ever truly becoming financially free.

And how could we, since as a generation we were lacking in even the basic tools of money management? Schools failed to teach even rudimentary personal finance. I remember taking a Russian history class in high school. This was in the early 1970s, during the Cold War. The reason being, I guess, if there ever was a Communist invasion, we would at least understand their culture! I used to say this at my workshops and people cracked up. The school system offered Russian history, but not one semester of personal finance! Was the government trying to keep us broke and stupid? I used to ask, "How many of you have ever had a class on personal finance? Learned how to balance a checkbook, prepare a tax return, fill out a loan application or run a profit and loss statement?" Few, if any, ever raised their hands. It wasn't until recently that the Commonwealth of Virginia made at least one semester of personal finance mandatory. Perhaps my griping during my radio shows and workshops got back to a politician somewhere.

It wasn't until 2003 that I discovered a way to generate a secure retirement revenue stream in a risky and challenging market. My good friend and longtime associate Merle Gilley, who I'd worked with on other successful ventures, called me about a new type of life insurance, called equity indexed universal (EIUL), that was just starting to attract attention.

At first it sounded too good to be true. Not only did it provide risk- and tax-free access to your money in the future, but the average rates of return were in the 8 percent range! After six months of research, I decided to fund an EIUL myself and then, if it delivered as promised, I would start offering them to the general public.

Of course, as with any new venture, there was a lot to learn. I worked with Merle to learn the product inside and out, sitting in on about 100 client meetings, where he would educate them, and if they were ready to move ahead, he would get them started. His mentoring greatly accelerated my success. Merle reinforced what I had already learned: Take care of clients, they will tell others and then you will have more clients than you can handle. Do the wrong thing, lose their money, and they will also spread the word and sooner or later you will be a failure.

As the old saying goes, if you follow the masses, you will end up just like them. However, the strategies discussed in this book have been used by the wealthy for years. So if you follow what works to create wealth, you too will have a much better chance to do the same.

Three Key Principles

The mere thought of retirement can be intimidating and confusing, raising a number of seemingly overwhelming questions. Will you outlive your retirement income? How much of it will be used to pay taxes? Should you add stocks, bonds and life insurance to your portfolio? Are your financial projections realistic?

Retirement Money Wave will help you boost your retirement wealth without risk or taxes and grow your nest egg by addressing three key areas:

1. Are you putting away enough money?

2. Do you have your money in the right accounts?

3. Have you considered the impact of taxes on your retirement wealth?

Question 1: Are you putting away enough money? Save more to have more.

Many people believe they can close shortfalls in their retirement savings by working a few extra years. In fact, according to a 2009 survey by the Employee Benefit Research Institute, more than one in four workers had changed their planned retirement ages; of these, 89 percent postponed retirement.

But what if you don't want to put off your retirement for a few years or, worse yet, are unable to continue working because of poor health or career problems? Even if you wouldn't mind staying on the job, consider the diminishing effects of time. Retirement contributions made during your last few years of work will have less time to grow than contributions made long before retirement.

The other solution to a retirement savings shortfall is so simple you might never have given it serious consideration: *Set aside more of your current income.* Even if you believe you are currently saving as much as possible toward retirement, you might change your mind after you run the numbers.

If everyone knows that they should be saving more money, why don't they? Americans have the "I want it now" mentality. They think, "I will worry about the cost or damage to my finances later, and retirement is years away." Most people tell themselves they will make it up in the future.

A better way to "have your cake and eat it too" would be to understand that the way you have been paying for cars, insurance, and homes, as well as your cash output in general, has been flawed. The deck is stacked against you by the banks and finance companies. Americans struggle to save 10 percent of their incomes, but what happens to the other 90 percent? Have you ever wondered where your paycheck goes? You put it into your account and it vanishes like magic.

Consider, for example, the mortgage on your house. The interest on a 30 year fixed mortgage for the average person is more than they will fund into their 401k account, both annually and over the course of their lifetime. Once you learn how these financial tools work, and the power of compounding money, it will become easier for you to accrue wealth. For example, trading cars in more often then you need to can harm your bottom line.

Decreasing your current consumption may not sound like much fun, but if you are looking forward to retirement, it could be less painful than working longer. The sooner you meet your retirement savings goals, the more choices you'll have when you do decide to leave work.

Question 2: Do you have your money in the right accounts? Find your balance.

If you've ever invested anything, especially in recent years, you're intimately acquainted with market volatility. Even though the S&P 500 had an 8.2 percent average annual return from 1990- 2009, the index has still seen some remarkable gains and losses. What people don't realize is the market gain over the last ten years is virtually zero percent! This lost decade is no way to build a secure retirement.

One way to help manage volatility is through asset allocation. However, the process of determining the appropriate proportion of assets based on your financial goals, risk tolerance and time horizon is hardly a set-it-and-forget-it strategy. Once you have implemented your preferred asset allocation, you'll need to monitor it and make sure it's growing properly.

Over time, performance of the different investments in your portfolio will invariably cause your allocation to change. Taking time to periodically rebalance — that is, to buy or sell investments to bring your asset mix in line with your target allocation — may help you be in a better position to pursue long-term goals. Rebalancing can help you stick to your investment strategy. It may also help you avoid the pitfalls of market timing, chasing performance and overexposing your portfolio to one asset class.

In the process of rebalancing your portfolio, you may incur commission costs as well as taxes if you sell investments for a profit. Therefore, you may want to rebalance less frequently; usually about once a year. However, you may also want to rebalance whenever the percentage of an asset class rises above a certain threshold, say 5-10 percent over your preferred asset allocation, or if your risk tolerance changes due to financial issues. But, with the equity indexed universal life insurance (EIUL) policy that I have researched and invested in, and will be discussing throughout this book, you may not need to rebalance; especially since neither stocks, bonds nor mutual funds are being traded. And remember that asset allocation is no guarantee against investment loss. It only helps manage investment risk.

 ## "BUCKETS" OF MONEY

When thinking about managing your money, consider placing it into "buckets." The first "bucket" would be would be short-term products for safe and liquid money, such as cash, checking and money market accounts and CDs. Accessibility, rather than rate of return, is the main concern; these are funds for emergencies such as car maintenance, house repairs and other unexpected bills.

The second "bucket" is what I call the intermediate, or 2-5 year "bucket", typically used to replenish funds used from various savings vehicles. Because it's being locked away for a while, you can expect to receive a higher rate of return than from savings or money market accounts. Intermediate bucket funds include short-term "fixed annuities" from safe and highly rated insurance companies. Like CDs, they offer fixed rates of return for a fixed period of time but actually provide an even higher return rate. For example, rather than paying a 1.7 percent return on a five year CD, some insurance companies offer a 3.4 percent return over the same period of time.

The third and final "bucket" is for the long term. These are the equity indexed universal life and/ or equity indexed annuities, and offer even higher rates of return without risk. These are monies to be used for retirement and are discussed in detail throughout this book.

Question 3: Have you considered the impact of taxes on your retirement wealth?

You have to consider the taxes. If you're funding a 401(k) or an IRA, you're creating a tax time bomb. Now, if you've got a few hundred dollars in your 401(k) it's no big deal. But if you've got a lifetime of savings, be it several hundred thousand or a couple of million, it could be a challenge in the future.

Socking away all your money into tax-deferred plans such as 401(k)s, 403(b)s, 457 plans and deductible IRAs can be good up, to a point. That point ends when you create a situation where all your financial nest eggs are in one tax-deductible basket or, as I like to say, "Tax me later at possibly a much higher rate." This can cause problems once you're retired because of how retirement income is taxed. Uncle Sam wants his cut. When you withdraw money from tax-deferred accounts, it will all be taxed as ordinary income in the calendar year in which you take the withdrawal.

Summary

You only have three places to build and deposit money for tax-free access in the future. They include: 1) a Roth IRA, 2) municipal bonds and 3) a life insurance contract. That's it; there are no other places to put tax-free money. This book will explain each of these and show you how to maximize your retirement wealth by following a simple, virtually risk-free strategy.

You can create your own personal Retirement Money Wave by using these three simple principles – putting away enough money, having it in the right accounts, and protecting your assets and your wealth from taxes.

Part 1: The Growing Storm

The Week Everything Changed: The Market Crash of 2008

A number of factors contributed to the stock market crash of October 2008. I discuss some of them below.

The Credit Market Collapse

The years before the credit market collapse provided fertile ground for the subprime mortgage industry. Individuals with poor credit were given access to loans they couldn't really afford. But as long as home prices were on the rise, poor lending practices were simply ignored.

Lenders could afford to give out bad loans as long as equity in the house outpaced the homeowner's desire for new debt. If borrowers failed to pay back their loans, lenders could always foreclose on the home, since it was an asset with ever-increasing value.

Problems began when housing prices started to fall in 2007. Homeowners increasingly found themselves with what are known as underwater loans; that is, they owed lenders more than the home was worth. As a result, homeowners no longer feared the threat of foreclosure. Even more disturbing was the fact that many families abandoned their homes and chose to start their lives anew in a different location, rather than worry about paying off their debts. More commonly, people who could no longer afford their mortgage stopped paying it until the banks foreclosed, and then they were evicted.

Bear Stearns' Collapse

As mortgage defaults rose, the economy began to falter, and fear crept into the credit markets. Despite the efforts of the Federal Reserve, the destabilization of the credit market quickly spread to the national financial system. Lenders began to fear borrowers could no longer repay their loans.

Bear Stearns was the first investment bank to fall prey to this unease. Investors, as well as other financial institutions, worried that their money would fail to be repaid and began pulling back their money.

On March 13, 2008, Bear Stearns advised the Federal Reserve that its liquidity position had deteriorated, and that it would be forced to file for bankruptcy unless they could find alternative sources of funds. Two days later, Bear Stearns agreed to merge with JP Morgan Chase in a deal that wiped out 90 percent of Bear Stearns' market value.

The Fall of Fannie Mae and Freddie Mac

Additionally, by 2008, the Federal National Mortgage Association (FNMA or Fannie Mae) and the Federal Home Loan Mortgage Corporation (FHLMC or Freddie Mac) either owned or had guaranteed nearly **$6 trillion** in mortgage loans. With the mortgage crisis brewing, these two corporations quickly began showing signs of financial distress. On September 7, the governing authority over these two agencies, the Federal Housing Finance Agency (FHFA) placed both Fannie Mae and Freddie Mac under their conservatorship. In addition, the U.S. Treasury began supplying funds to help stabilize them, therefore raising the national debt ceiling by $800 billion.

Financial Instability Grows

On September 14, a second wave of volatility began in the financial community when Bank of America agreed to acquire Merrill Lynch for $50 billion. On September 15, market instability was further exacerbated by concerns over the ability of financial institutions to cover their exposure in both the subprime loan market as well as credit default swaps. That same day, Lehman Brothers was forced to file for Chapter 11 bankruptcy protection.

On September 16, the American International Group (AIG) also fell victim to a liquidity crisis, as their shares lost 95 percent of their value and the company reported a $13.2 billion loss in the first six months of the year. By September 22, AIG had been removed from the Dow Jones Industrial Average (DJIA) and was replaced by Kraft Foods.

Although history may state the actual market crash occurred on Monday, October 6, prior to that date it experienced eight consecutive trading days of negative movement. Table 1.1 shows the DJIA decline from October 1-10.

Date, 2008	DJIA Close	Point Change	Percent Change
October 1	10,831.07	-19.59	-0.18%
October 2	10,482.85	-348.22	-3.22%
October 3	10,325.38	-157.47	-1.50%
October 6	9,955.50	-369.88	-3.58%
October 7	9,447.11	-508.39	-5.11%
October 8	9,258.10	-189.01	-2.00%
October 9	8,579.19	-678.91	-7.33%
October 10	8,451.19	-128.00	-1.49%

Table 1.1. Over the Precipice: The Dow Jones Industrial Average (DJIA) Drop

During those eight trading days, the DJIA dropped a total of 2,399.47 points, or 22.11 percent. The market rebounded sharply on Monday, October 13, rising 936.42 points, only to drop 733.08 points two days later on Wednesday.

October was shaping up to be a volatile month, as investors began reacting to the worrisome credit market news that had started back in March.

The Crash of 2008 Begins

Although the market arguably started its crash on October 1, Black Week began on October 6th and lasted five trading sessions. During that time, the DJIA plummeted 1,874 points or 18.1 percent. That same week, the S&P 500 fell more than 20 percent.

After a brief uptick in mid-October, the market started a second decline. On October 24, the Dow plunged 312.30 points to 8,378.95, its lowest level since April 25, 2003. The S&P 500 dropped 31.24 points to 876.77, its biggest drop since April 11, 2003. Finally, the NASDAQ Composite tumbled 51.88 points to 1,552.03, its largest fall since May 23, 2003.

Summary

A number of underlying issues had threatened the economy before that first week in October. In addition to the above-mentioned foreclosures and declining home values, there was a growing national debt, bankruptcies, threats of increasing inflation, municipal bond defaults and increased taxes.

After Black Week, many people realized that things had to change. No longer could we ignore the obvious fact that the emperor had no clothes – to do so would vresult in financial peril, not to mention overexposure. It was time to figure out a way to achieve real financial security.

The Lost Decade

If you think saving and investing your retirement money in stocks will produce a secure financial future, you may be wrong – especially if the last decade repeats itself (see Figure 1.1). The Dow Jones Industrial Average (DJIA) right now is about at the same level as it was on January

14, 2000. What this means is that we've lost *one decade of potential investment growth*.

The Loss that Keeps on Giving

Figure 1.1 illustrates the zero-growth stock market that took place between 2001-10. A lost decade, or something akin to it, could feel like a never-ending recession to many Americans, as a stalled economy fails to recoup lost jobs. Investments like homes and stocks also continue to lose value.

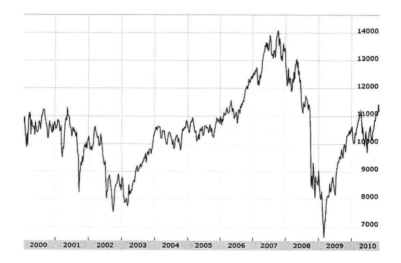

Figure 1.1. Zero Sum Game – DJIA Closing Numbers from 2001-11

Another "lost decade" occurred in Japan in the 1990s. From 1992-99, the Japanese economy grew by less than 1 percent a year. It has yet to fully recover from the economic weaknesses and falling prices of that period. And, it is now entering its third decade of a recession undoubtedly made worse by the recent tragic earthquake, tsunami and nuclear power plant failures.

Disasters aside, a number of economic similarities exist between Japan in the 1990s and the United States today. Japan's real estate bubble inflated and then burst, resulting in banks being choked with bad loans and causing a subsequent cutback in lending.

And there's more to our economic downturn than meets the eye. While the housing market has dropped precipitously, unemployment has risen, and the national debt continues to mount into the trillions of dollars, there is another, more permanent factor that is delaying recovery. Just as in Japan, the aging population is growing exponentially. More people are collecting benefits from programs like Social Security, with fewer paying in to support the outflow. Additionally, consumers are holding onto their money, borrowing and spending less. Some investors are putting money into commodities or stocks in foreign countries like Brazil, Russia, India and China, while baby boomers concerned about retirement look to invest in Treasury bonds and mutual funds which seem to provide guaranteed returns. None of these factors bode well for growing the economy.

401(k)s Become 201(k)s

So what is a 201(k)? Rather than being a new type of investment account, it's actually how many individual investors feel after watching their 401(k) balances drop by 30, 40 and even 50 percent starting in the fall of 2008; hence, the term "201(k)." Corporate America convinced millions of people that the 401(k) plan was a good replacement for the traditional retirement plans their parents had enjoyed for decades. So we bought into the lie and went along with the idea. If you put your life savings into a 401(k) program, you may have watched it decline by as much as half.

Foreclosures and Dropping Home Values

In the past, increased home values funded retirement plans and offered homeowners easy credit for everything from exotic vacations to luxury cars to flat-screen TVs. As most of us are painfully aware, the days of big spending and huge lines of credit are over.

In November 2010, U.S. home prices fell for the 53rd consecutive month, surpassing even the percentage of home price decline during the Great Depression. Home prices were at their peak in June 2006, after which the slump began (see Figure 1.2). Since then, they have fallen over 26 percent, exceeding the 25.9 percent drop registered in the five years between 1928-33, according to Zillow.com, an online real estate database.

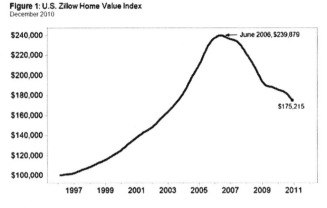

Figure 1: U.S. Zillow Home Value Index
December 2010

Figure 1.2. Zillow Home Value Index (Dec. 2010)

(Source: Zillow.com)

It is a dubious milestone for the U.S. housing market, which has since failed to gain much traction despite a host of government programs to reduce delinquencies and encourage demand with temporary tax credits and lower interest rates. Many economists expect further price drops, despite anecdotal signs of growing demand, such as pending home sales data.

When the easy money of home equity dries up with declining home values, it leaves borrowers with little choice. Credit card balances balloon for many, which can lead to tapping credit limits, late charges and missed payments, including mortgage payments. This cascade of debt has led to an avalanche of home foreclosures (see Figure 1.3).

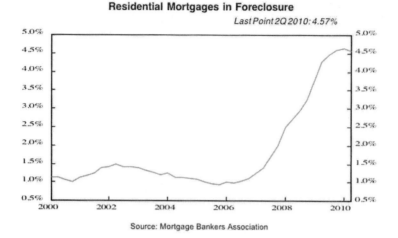

Residential Mortgages in Foreclosure

Last Point 2Q 2010: 4.57%

Source: Mortgage Bankers Association

Figure 1.3. Residential Mortgages in Foreclosure
(Source: Mortgage Bankers Association)

And another housing bubble is getting ready to pop. Millions of adjustable rate mortgages (ARMs) taken out over the last ten years are due to reset over the next several months. This means that homeowners could be stuck with "balloon" payments, which can be as much as double what they're paying now. While some banks are taking steps that allow homeowners to refinance, not all qualify, and many more may go into foreclosure.

Growing National Debt

Our national debt now tops $14.5 trillion. And we're paying a trillion dollars in interest a year and must borrow money from other countries just to keep our heads above water financially. As a result, the United States is no longer the only super power; countries such as India, China and Brazil are catching up. This is because, as a nation, we're mismanaging our money like many of our citizens have done over the last few decades (see Figure 1.4).

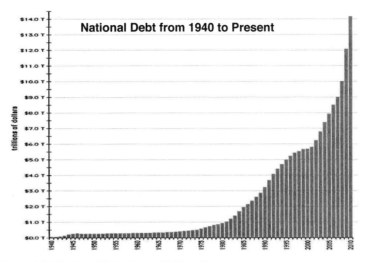

Figure 1.4. National Debt from 1940 to Present
(Source: U.S. National Debt Clock; http://brillig.com/debt_clock/)

What's A Trillion Dollars?

So what does a trillion dollars look like? Ten thousand dollars worth of $100 bills would be about an inch thick.

A million dollars would look like this:

Now, if you had a $100 million, it'd be a pile of dough.

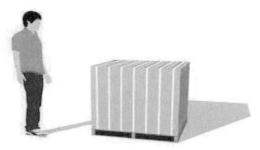

Not too bad. A billion dollars, we're getting a little bit bigger.

A trillion dollars... the pallets are double stacked – and these are $100 bills. Now that's a mind-blowing pile of money!

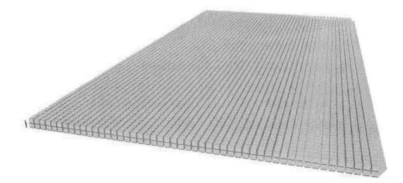

In other words, if a billion dollars is 10 pallets of $100 bills, a trillion is 10,000 pallets!

We have $111 trillion worth of unfunded liabilities, promises that were made generations ago. These include Social Security, Medicare, and Part D Medicare Prescription. The latter alone has added another $19 trillion, while Medicare has contributed $80 trillion, and that's not even counting some of the recent add-ons to that plan.

Bottom line: Our debt is out of control and will overtake everything unless we get a handle on it.

Bankruptcies

No surprise here – Bankruptcies are on the rise in our declining economy. Unfortunately, bankruptcy may be the only option for someone with thousands of dollars of credit card debt, zero or negative home equity and/or who lost their job. Even if you manage your money responsibly, you can make poor or uninformed investment decisions (see Figure 1.5).

Figure 1.5. U.S. Daily Bankruptcy Filings, Jan. 2006-Feb.2009

The Return of Inflation

When the stock market dives, people contemplating retirement or who are already retired often take their money out of the market and put it into a seemingly safe CD. Over the past couple of years, the national CD rates have been about 1.57 percent, a dramatic drop from the 5 percent average over the last 50 years.

And what about inflation? There hasn't been any, because prices have been falling on everything from houses to cars to mortgages. We're in a deflationary period, and just about everything's on sale!

Over time, inflation has averaged about 3 percent. So what does that mean? That means if I retire, I might take all my money out of an IRA and roll it over into a CD because I think I'm going to get a certain guaranteed percentage and won't lose money anymore. In fact, if I get lucky and things improve, I might get a 2-4 percent return on my investment.

But what happens when inflation comes back? Didn't that just wipe out your gains? Oh, and what about the taxes that come due once you cash that CD?

While it may appear that you're accumulating wealth by putting money into CDs, the truth is a lot murkier. For one thing, the price of everything doubles about every 14-16 years, so any gains will disappear quickly and you'll eventually run out of funds. So, if you think gasoline, milk and bread prices are high now, wait another decade or so. You can compensate for inflation while you're still working by taking on longer hours or a second job, but what do you do when you're retired?

Most people think that a deflationary period will be followed by inflation. And to some extent this is already happening with gasoline and grocery prices. Between growing economies such as India, China and Brazil, and the unrest and instability in the Middle East, which contributes to extreme fluctuations in oil prices, inflation seems inevitable. For example, consider internet airfares. One minute, they're $200, then in a half-hour, it's gone up to $350! Why? Fuel prices. Those higher fuel prices are also going to increase the cost of getting goods to stores. And these costs will be passed to us, the consumers.

In a struggling economy, there is rising inflation. And that's going to put major roadblocks on the road to recovery.

Municipal Defaults

States and local governments raise money by issuing municipal bonds. Throughout the U.S., these entities are now struggling under the weight of their budget woes. As a result, even these bonds may be at risk, especially in

STEVE SAYS

Understanding your mortgage helps create wealth. Failure to do so may prevent you from achieving your financial goals. The average American homeowner will pay hundreds of thousands up to a million dollars in interest alone on their mortgage.

hard-hit places like California, Illinois, Michigan, New York or New Jersey.

Municipal bond defaults could go up to as much as $100 billion over the next five years, according to a new estimate from Roubini Global Economics. The game has changed, and what was once a secure source of return might no longer be a solid investment.

Summary

Our economy is in big trouble and there are only two ways to fix it: 1) cut spending or 2) raise taxes. What do you think raising taxes will do to your future retirement plans? The reality is you need to learn the new rules of protecting and growing your retirement and plan for your future accordingly. One way to begin is by examining a short history of retirement plans.

Part 2: A Short History of Retirement Plans

Social Security, Mother of All Retirement Plans

In 2011, more than 54 million Americans will receive $730 billion in Social Security benefits. This presents a significant increase over 2010 (see Table 2.1).

DECEMBER 2010 BENEFICIARY DATA			
Retired workers	35 million	$40.7 billion	$1,175 average monthly benefit
Dependents	2.9 million	$1.7 billion	
Disabled workers	8 million	$8.8 billion	$1,068 average monthly benefit
Dependents	2 million	$.6 billion	
Survivors	6.4 million	$6.3 billion	$1,134 average monthly benefit

Table 2.1 Social Security Data

According to the Congressional Budget Office (CBO), Social Security's outlays will exceed its tax revenue every year through 2021. In doing so, it will add $626 billion to the federal deficit from 2010-16, with a total of $1.361 trillion from 2010-21. To paraphrase Batman, holy liability!

 ## Background and History

PROMISES, PROMISES

Democratic President Franklin Delano Roosevelt (FDR) introduced the Social Security program in 1935. He promised:

- That participation in the program would be completely voluntary.

- That the participants would only have to pay 1 percent of the first $1,400 of their annual incomes into the program.

- That the money the participants elected to put into the program would be tax deductible.

- That participants would put money into an independent "Trust Fund" rather than into the General Operating Fund used for other government programs. "Trust Fund" money was solely designated for Social Security retirement and no other program.

- That the annuity payments to the retirees would never be taxed as income.

  Look what happened to these promises. So how did the current situation come to be?

Social Security has its origins in ancient Britain. When the colonists arrived in North America, they were steeped in their homeland's notions and practices, including the so-called Poor Laws, which emulated the Elizabethan Poor Law of 1601. In the early days of the United States, these laws made a distinction between those who were unable to work due to age or physical health and those who were able-bodied but unemployed. The first group was assisted with cash or alternative forms of help from the government, while the second group was given public service employment in workhouses.

In general, however, American attitudes toward poverty relief were usually haphazard, so governmental involvement was slight. Throughout the 1800s, there were some attempts at reform to help them move to work rather than continuing to need assistance. Social casework, consisting of visits to the poor to train them in morals and a work ethic, was advocated by reformers in the 1880s and '90s.

Social Security as we know it today did not actually come into being until 1935, but there was one significant predecessor, a post-Civil war program intended for hundreds of thousands of disabled veterans and their widows and orphans. This led to the creation of a pension plan with some similarities to present-day Social Security.

But in fact, most early American families cared for their own, so when someone became elderly or disabled, the last place they looked for help was the government. However, certain trends in the 19th century made conventional ways of securing economic survival increasingly obsolete. They included:

- The Industrial Revolution

- A population shift from the countryside to cities

- Longer life expectancy

- The diminishment of the extended family

Americans had become increasingly industrialized, citified and older, and fewer people lived near their relatives.

The Social Security Act and Its Subsequent Amendments

On August 14, 1935, the Social Security Act became law. One of the truly momentous legislative accomplishments in U.S. history, it was enacted in the throes of the Great Depression. A sweeping bill that generated an array of programs to aid numerous groups of Americans, the law got its title from the groundbreaking program designed to provide a steady income for retired workers aged 65 or older.

The Social Security Act signifies a sharp departure from prior American tradition. The United States had customarily stressed "pulling oneself up by the bootstraps" and voluntarism to alleviate social ills. Prior to 1929, the federal government didn't furnish such programs as old-age pensions, public assistance, unemployment compensation or health insurance — except for war veterans.

However, the Depression of the early 1930s generated nationwide misery and sparked a popular crusade for old-age pensions coordinated by a retired California doctor, Francis Townsend. The Roosevelt administration responded by establishing the Social Security Act in 1935. The program would basically be funded by payroll or taxes (Social Security payroll taxes are collected under the authority of FICA, the Federal Insurance Contributions Act. These payroll taxes are sometimes even called "FICA taxes.").The Act has been amended numerous times, notably in 1939 when surviving spouses and minor children were included as beneficiaries. Subsequently, payroll/FICA taxes grew to subsidize this.

In the 1950s, more people were added to Social Security's beneficiary pool, and the benefit was increased, including the first cost-of-living allowance (COLA) since 1940. In 1956, disability insurance was instituted and augmented over subsequent years. Early retirement for women at age 62 was permitted. Payroll taxes hovered at 4 percent.

◀ STEVE SAYS

You are the CEO of your own life. Because of that you'll need to have a budget, know where your money goes and try to improve your bottom line.

In 1961, early retirement for men at age 62 was allowed. Once again, payroll taxes rose to 6 percent. A major advance occurred when the Social Security Administration was charged with providing healthcare to beneficiaries aged 65 or older, under the new Medicare Act signed into law by President Lyndon B. Johnson on July 30, 1965. The Health Care Financing Administration (HCFA) now maintains Medicare.

In 1972 the law was modified to provide a yearly COLA, keyed to the annual increase in consumer prices, to begin in 1975.

Concerns about the Social Security system's financial health surfaced in the 1980s. In 1983, President Ronald Reagan signed into law, for the first time, the taxation of Social Security benefits. In addition, coverage was extended to federal employees, the retirement age was to be raised beginning in 2000, and the reserves in the Social Security Trust Funds were increased. In 1985, the Social Security Trust Funds were moved out of the federal budget so that funds set aside for the Social Security system could be tracked separately. By then, payroll taxes were pegged at 11.4 percent.

In 1993, the amount of taxable benefits for upper income retirees was increased to 85 percent and payroll taxes rose to 12.4 percent. In 1996, the Social Security Trustees' Report stated that the system would begin to go into the red in 2012, and the trust funds would peter out by 2029. All members of the trustees' advisory panel concurred that at least some Social Security funds should be invested in the private sector. To keep the system as it was and actuarially sound, they wrote, payroll taxes would have to rise by 50 percent or benefits would have to be cut by 30 percent.

In 1999, the Social Security Trustees' Report stated that the Social Security Retirement System's unfunded liability increased by $752 billion since the 1998 Trustee Report was released. That brought the total long-term unfunded liability to more than $19 trillion. In 2000, President Bill Clinton signed into law H.R. 5, "The Senior Citizens' Freedom to Work Act of 2000," which allowed approximately 900,000 officially retired but employed beneficiaries to keep their benefits without reductions. And, primarily due to the aging Baby Boomer population, the money from Social Security keeps rolling out, while much less is being taken in due to an increasingly smaller population who are of working age.

Social Security in a Nutshell

According to the Social Security Administration (SSA), the trends listed in the following section occurred in 2009:

- Social Security is the major source of income for most of the elderly.

- Nine out of ten individuals age 65 and older receive Social Security benefits.

- Social Security benefits represent about 41 percent of the income of the elderly.

- Among elderly Social Security beneficiaries, 54 percent of married couples and 73 percent of unmarried persons receive 50 percent or more of their income from Social Security.

- Among elderly Social Security beneficiaries, 22 percent of married couples and about 43 percent of unmarried persons rely on Social Security for 90 percent or more of their income.

Social Security provides more than just retirement benefits:

- Retired workers and their dependents account for 69 percent of total benefits paid.

- Disabled workers and their dependents account for 19 percent of total benefits paid.

  - About 91 percent of workers ages 21-64 in covered employment and their families have protection in the event of a long-term disability.

  - Just over one in four of today's 20 year-olds will become disabled before reaching age 67.

  - 67 percent of the private sector workforce has no long-term disability insurance.

◀ STEVE SAYS

Tax free is better than tax deferred. While it may seem attractive to defer paying taxes on money saved for retirement because you're in a lower tax bracket now, how high do you think your taxes will be when you do cash in that retirement?

- Survivors of deceased workers account for about 12 percent of total benefits paid.

  - About one in eight of today's 20 year-olds will die before reaching age 67.

  - About 97 percent of persons ages 20-49 who worked in covered employment have survivor's insurance protection for their young children and the surviving spouse caring for the children.

Social Security covers a huge amount of pending retirees:

- An estimated 158 million workers, some 94 percent, are covered under Social Security.

  - 50 percent of the workforce has no private pension coverage.

  - 31 percent of the workforce has no savings set aside specifically for retirement.

- In 1935, the life expectancy of a 65-year-old was 12½ years, today it's 18 years.

- By 2041, there will be almost twice as many older Americans as today – from 41.6 million today to 79.1 million.

- There are currently 2.9 workers for each Social Security beneficiary. By 2041, there will be 2.1 workers for each beneficiary.

Monthly Benefits Add Up

The payments of monthly Social Security benefits began in January 1940, and were authorized not only for retired workers but also for their wives or widows as well as surviving parents of a certain age and children under the age of 18.

On January 31, 1940, the first monthly retirement check was issued to Ida May Fuller of Ludlow, Vermont, in the amount of $22.54. Miss Fuller, a legal secretary, retired in November 1939. She started collecting benefits in January 1940 at age 65 and lived to be 100 years old, dying in 1975.

Ida May Fuller worked for three years under the Social Security program. The accumulated taxes on her salary during those three years totaled $24.75. Her initial monthly check was $22.54. During her lifetime she collected a total of $22,888.92 in Social Security benefits. That's quite a profit for her investment!

Summary

While the only retirement, medical and disability plan for many Americans, Social Security has become a major drain on our economy and government; one which will only increase. With few easy fixes in sight, this program's future is hardly "secure," so plan accordingly.

Retirement Alphabet Soup:
401(k)s, IRAs/Roth IRAs, TSPs and More, Oh My!

A number of retirement plans are available to supplement or, in some cases, replace Social Security. They can represent an overwhelming alphabet soup of choices, so it's best to investigate them thoroughly. Along with 401(k)s, there are IRAs and Simple IRAs, SEPs and TSPs, among others.

401(k) Plans

In 1978, Congress decided that Americans needed some encouragement to put aside money for retirement. An incentive might be to give them a way to save while at the same time lowering their state and federal taxes.

Created by the Revenue Act of 1978, the 401(k) retirement tax-deferred savings plan is named after section 401, paragraph (k) of the Internal Revenue Service tax code. The 401(k) is for employees who work in the private sector or for nonprofit organizations. Contributions can be made with pre-tax earnings.

Ted Benna, a benefits consultant, came up with the first version of this plan and proposed regulations were issued in 1981. In 1982, taxpayers were able to take advantage of the 401(k) for the first time.

401(k) plans are part of a family of retirement plans known as defined contribution plans, so named because the amount contributed is defined either by the employee (a.k.a. the participant) or the employer.

IRAs / Roth IRAs

Introduced in 1974, Individual Retirement Accounts (IRAs) were a part of the Employee Retirement Income Security Act (ERISA) of 1974. Enacted to protect the interests of employee benefit plan participants and their beneficiaries, ERISA establishes minimum standards for pension plans in private industry and provides for extensive rules on the federal income tax effects of transactions associated with employee benefit plans.

The act allowed an employee to contribute $1,500 each year into an IRA. The Individual Retirement Accounts created in 1974 constitute traditional IRAs; in addition, Simple IRAs and Roth IRAs are now available for funding retirement.

Employer retirement plans

IRAs were unavailable to individuals with qualified employment-based retirement plans, however. If you had another retirement account or plan provided by your employer, you could not contribute to IRA accounts.

But in 1981, under the Economic Recovery Tax Act, the law was changed to allow anyone under 70½ years of age to contribute to an IRA, with the maximum contribution set at $2,000 and $250 for nonworking spouses. In 1996, the Simple IRA, which allowed employers to match contributions into an IRA account, was added to the portfolio for small businesses.

Established by the Taxpayer Relief Act of 1997, the Roth IRA allows taxpayers, subject to certain income limits, to save for retirement while allowing the savings to grow tax-free. Taxes are paid on contributions, but withdrawals, subject to certain rules, are not taxed at all. Contributions to the Roth IRA are invested in mutual funds, stocks or other securities, and the amount that someone contributes depends upon their income, age and tax filing status. Roth IRAs are unique in that they do not require you to start making withdrawals at a certain age, and also allow qualified withdrawals of up to $10,000 for a first-time home purchase.

Taxes

The amount contributed to an IRA at or below the maximum yearly contribution becomes a tax deduction. The contributed amount is subtracted from the gross income before taxes are determined each year. IRA accounts have a tax-deferred status, and any contribution is not taxed until it is withdrawn from the account. This includes capital gains earned on any IRA investment. In 2006, withdrawals for charitable contributions became tax-free.

Contributions

A contributor must be self-employed or earning a taxable income to participate in an IRA. At the inception of IRA accounts, the maximum contribution was set at $1,500, and it was available only to individuals without an ERISA. In 2010, the maximum contribution was set at $5,000 per person, covered or not covered under an ERISA. These funds are contributed on a pre-tax basis for simple IRAs and an after-tax basis for Roth IRAs.

IRA summary

- Tax deductible contributions (depending on income level)

- Withdrawals begin at age 59½ and mandatory by 70½

- Taxes are paid on earnings when withdrawn from the IRA

- Funds can be used to purchase a variety of investments (stocks, bonds, certificates of deposits, etc.)

- Available to everyone; no income restrictions

- All funds withdrawn (including principal contributions) before 59½ are subject to a 10 percent penalty (subject to exception)

STEVE SAYS

Wealth lost includes taxes and interest on credit cards, mortgage and cars.... The way you pay for things can kill your chances for financial security.

Roth IRA summary

- Contributions are not tax deductible

- No mandatory distribution age

- All earnings and principal are 100 percent tax-free if rules and regulations are followed

- Funds can be used to purchase a variety of investments (stocks, bonds, certificates of deposits, etc.)

- Principal contributions can be withdrawn any time without penalty (subject to some minimal conditions)

Tax-deferred vs. tax-free

The biggest difference between the traditional and Roth IRA is the way the government treats the taxes. If you earn $50,000 a year and put $2,000 in a traditional IRA, you will be able to deduct the contribution from your income taxes (meaning you only have to pay tax on $48,000 in income to the IRS). At 59½, you may begin withdrawing funds but will have to pay taxes, whether it's on the principle or any earned capital gains, interest, dividends, etc.

On the other hand, if you put the same $2,000 in a Roth IRA, you would not receive the income tax deduction. If you needed the money in the account, you could withdraw the principal at any time (although there are penalties if you withdraw any earnings the money has made). When you reach retirement age, you can withdraw all of the money 100 percent tax-free.

Therefore, in most situations, a Roth IRA makes more sense. Unfortunately, not everyone qualifies, and it excludes singles earning more than $150,000 a year and married couples with a combined maximum income of $169,000.

Simplified Employee Pension Plans (SEPs)

A retirement program for self-employed people or owners of small companies, the Simplified Employee Pension plan (SEP) allows employers to contribute on behalf of eligible employees without the startup and operating costs of a conventional retirement plan. SEPs can provide a significant source of retirement income by allowing employers to set aside money in accounts for themselves and their employees. Under a SEP, an employer contributes directly to traditional individual retirement accounts (SEP-IRAs). Advantages include:

- Contributions to a SEP are tax deductible and your business pays no taxes on the earnings on the investments.

- Contributions can be integrated with Social Security contributions.

- You are not locked into making contributions every year. In fact, you decide each year whether, and then how much, to contribute to your employees' SEP-IRAs. The SEP allows for a contribution of up to 25 percent of each employee's pay.

- Generally, you do not have to file any documents with the government.

- Sole proprietors, partnerships and corporations, including S corporations, can set up SEPs.

- You may be eligible for a tax credit of up to $500 per year for each of the first 3 years for the cost of starting the plan.

- Administrative costs are low.

Thrift Savings Plans (TSPs)

Sponsored by the federal government, the thrift savings plan (TSP) is a defined contribution for United States civil service employees and retirees as well as for members of the uniformed services. It is also open to employees covered under the older Civil Service Retirement System (CSRS). Because TSPs were designed to closely resemble the dynamics of private sector 401(k) plans with many of the same type of savings and tax benefits, your TSP retirement income will depend on how much you have contributed during your working years, and the earnings on those contributions.

The TSP is one of three components of the Federal Employees Retirement System (FERS). The other two are the FERS annuity and Social Security.

Congress established the TSP in the Federal Employees' Retirement System Act of 1986. On October 30, 2000, the Floyd D. Spence National Defense Authorization Act for Fiscal Year 2001 (Public Law 106-398) was also signed into law, extending participation in the TSP to members of the uniformed services.

Among other things, benefits of the TSPs include the following:

- Immediate member contributions
- A choice of whether to participate and how much to contribute
- Before-tax savings and tax-deferred investment earnings
- Daily valuation of accounts
- Low administrative and investment expenses
- Transfers into the TSP from other eligible retirement plans or traditional IRAs and eligible employer plans
- A selection of investment funds
- Ability to make contribution allocations daily
- Ability to make inter-fund transfers daily
- Loans from your own contributions and attributable earnings while you are in service
- Catch-up contributions for participants age 50 or older
- In-service withdrawals for financial hardship or after you reach age 59½
- Portable benefits and a choice of withdrawal options after you separate from service

Summary

While useful, knowledge of retirement plans will only take you so far in understanding why your savings may be at risk. The following sections will show you how to protect and use your savings to your advantage and subsequently allow you to retire with wealth.

Part 3: The Baby Boomerang Effect

Economy, Debt and an Aging Population

The baby boom after the end of World War II launched an economic and social phenomenon that would define several generations. On January 1, 2011, the first wave of America's 78 million baby boomers began turning 65 at the rate of about 10,000 per day. And if past experience is any indication, when those born between 1946-64 reach age 65, it will redefine what it means to be a senior.

A Landmark Year

2011 marks the beginning of retirement for many baby boomers, and while it sounds like cause for celebration, there are several major problems. Neither employers nor the government has the money to fund a full retirement, nor do the boomers. According to the Census Bureau, there are more than 78 million boomers in the U.S. and by 2030, this demographic (born between 1946-64) will represent an estimated 20 percent of the population. So more than 10,000 baby boomers will turn 65 every day for the next 19 years.

Experts agree that funding retirement for boomers will be much more challenging than anticipated. Not only because of the financial shortfalls, but also because of the amount of years individuals will no longer be working. Extended retirement wasn't even a consideration when Social Security was established in the 1930s and life expectancies were much shorter. Monthly Social Security payments will still provide some income, but without other investments, it will be nearly impossible to exist on that alone. Additionally, the cost of health care continues to rise significantly.

The picture has changed dramatically since boomers saw their parents enter their so-called golden years. And the next generation – the children of boomers – are adding their own complications. More than half of baby boom-generation mothers support adult children financially and 60 percent are the go-to person when their grown kids encounter problems. That's a sharp contrast from the 86 percent of 46-65 year-old women who were fully independent of their own parents by age 25, accordingto the Center for Economic and Policy Research.

The "Boomer"-ang Effect

With 78 million baby boomers moving from a consumption state to one of conservation, the markets still need cash to make them function and grow. As a "common sense economist", which means I have no formal training other than years of being in business, and because I remember the lessons of Mom and Dad, if you spend more then you make or take in, eventually bad things will happen. Wall Street encourages people to buy stocks and wants you to believe that you need to be in the market and that the market will "always" comes back. That may be true over the long term, but no other nation in history has ever seen the amount of debt that we have racked up.

If the baby boomers finally wake up one day and realize it's time to live within their means, start saving and not maxing out every credit card they can get their hands on, this adds up to money that is not flowing through the system. They aren't eating out at restaurants as often, so the waitress doesn't have as many tips. The chef doesn't have as many dinners to cook, and the eatery has less revenue and may need to lay staff off. These people with less income cut back, and the funds that they would normally spend on haircuts, shopping for new clothes, cars, etc. is not there. These trillions of dollars in funds that now don't exist or are sitting in savings, instead of moving through the economy, begin to cause high unemployment, lower sales of everything, including tax revenue, and result in exploding the deficits in the federal, state and local government budgets. Unfortunately, this has already begun to occur and based on recent events, is likely to become more the norm.

We don't have the money. It simply isn't there. But the millions of baby boomers getting ready to retire are counting on it. This all comes at the worst possible time for a federal government that's almost flat broke and for a national economy already teetering on the brink of disaster. Let's look at some factors that have contributed to this pending crisis.

Declining Net Worth

In the past five years, boomers ages 46-54 have seen their average net worth decline by 45 percent, from $172,400 to $94,200. The older boomers have seen their net worth drop by nearly half, from $315,400 to $159,800; the wealth of the median household has fallen by almost 50 percent, from $315,400 in 2004 to $159,800 in 2009. With their working days numbered, many realize they can't recoup. Whether that means delaying retirement, learning new skills, or changing careers altogether, the staying-alive strategies of boomers – at 38 percent, the largest segment of the American workforce – leave younger workers wondering when or even if they'll get to move up the ladder.

Still, this net worth might be sufficient to cover approximately 90 percent of the cost of the typical house, if they had no other assets. However, as a result of plunging real estate prices, many people, including baby boomers, now have little or no equity in their home. Of those who own their primary residence, nearly 30 percent of households headed by someone between the ages 45-54 would need to bring money to a closing to cover their mortgage and transaction costs.

Decreased Savings

As the 78 million baby boomers head for retirement, they will be faced with the challenge of saving like they've never saved before. Figure 3.1 tracks the multi-decade decline of U.S. consumer saving habits. For the better part of a quarter century, Americans found less need to save with each passing year.

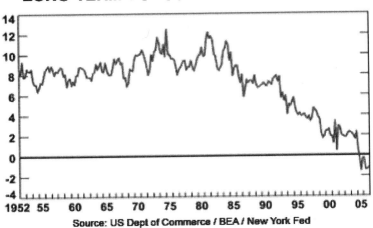

LONG-TERM CONSUMER SAVINGS RATE

Source: US Dept of Commerce / BEA / New York Fed

Figure 3.1 Long-term Consumer Savings Rate
(Source: U.S. Department of Commerce/BEA/New York Fed)

The flipside of this savings decline, of course, was an epic spending boom. People saved less because they bought more – all too often on credit. As the boom rolled on, credit lines were maxed out; we purchased as much "stuff" as we could get our hands on. The savings rate even went negative at the height of the housing bubble – not because people were feeling cash poor, but because homeowners across the land felt gloriously flush.

So, how are boomers going to manage their savings, and where are they going to put the money?

Consumer Debt Increasing

High consumer debt has a big impact on both your standard of living and your ability to ensure you have enough money for retirement. According to www.creditcards.com:

- Average credit card debt per household with credit card debt: $14,750

- 609.8 million credit cards held by U.S. consumers.

- Average number of credit cards held by cardholders: 3.5 as of year end 2008

- Average APR on new credit card offer: 14.73 percent

- Average APR on credit card with a balance on it: 13.67 percent as of November 2010

- Total U.S. revolving debt (98 percent of which is made up of credit card debt) – $796.5 billion as of November 2010

- Total U.S. consumer debt: $2.40 trillion as of June 2010

- U.S. credit card 60-day delinquency rate: 3.23 percent.

Figure 3.2 illustrates the astronomical rise of credit card debt.

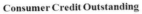

Consumer Credit Outstanding

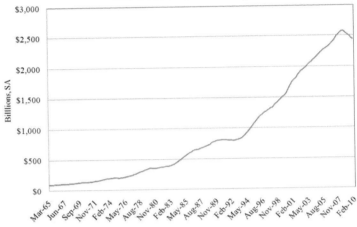

Figure 3.2. Consumer Credit
(Source: Federal Reserve Flow of Funds Accounts report)

Dropping Home Values

Traditionally, home equity has been a source of wealth and savings that funded retirement expenses. However, the real estate market bust and stock market declines have carved huge chunks out of the assets of baby boomers, so that many nearing retirement will have very little to live on.

In fact, so much home equity has been lost that, according to Fitch Ratings, 30 percent of boomers aged 45-54 are underwater in their homes. And 18 percent of boomers aged 55-64 would owe money at close if they sold their homes today. The Zillow Home Value Index chart on page 21 illustrates the dramatic drop in home values over the past few years.

The Center for Economic and Policy Research (CEPR) found that people who rented homes in 2004 would likely have more wealth in 2009 than those who owned.

That's true for all wealth groups, from the richest to the poorest. The collapse of the housing bubble, which led to the current recession, has already destroyed almost $6 trillion in wealth. Add this to the instability in the stock market, and many baby boomers will only have Social Security and Medicare to rely on in retirement.

Increased Health Care Expenses

Today America's elderly are living longer, and the cost of health care is rising dramatically. Those two factors combined will make senior healthcare incredibly expensive.

Boomers are expected to live longer than any previous generation of Americans. Of the 3.4 million born in 1946 – including Bill Clinton, George and Laura Bush, Donald Trump, Susan Sarandon, Steven Spielberg, and Sylvester Stallone – 2.8 million are still alive. The men can expect to live another 22 years, the women another 25.

By 2030, when the first baby boomers reach 84, the number of Americans over 65 will have grown by 75 percent to 69 million. That means more than 20 percent of the population will be over 65, compared with only 13 percent today. More than 35 percent will be over 50.

Will boomers stay healthy?

Today, baby boomers make up 26 percent of the U.S. population. A fragile, dependent population of aging boomers would place tremendous demands on their personal savings and Medicare and require lots of support from professional caregivers and their own families.

As with the rest of the population, obesity is another problem. According to the Department of Health and Human resources, the number of obese Americans 55-64 has jumped from 31 percent (1988-1994) to 39 percent (1999-2002). Widespread obesity, combined with lack of exercise, could lead to an epidemic of diabetes, heart problems and other chronic ailments which would dramatically accelerate aging and lead to increased healthcare costs.

Retirement Anxiety – The Baby Boomerang Effect

With retirement just on the horizon, many baby boomers are worried they'll lack the money to sail smoothly into their sunset years. And their fears are well founded; as they near the end of their careers, their savings have diminished and the economy is still struggling to recover.

The past decade has seen basically flat stock market returns, as well as low rates of return on bonds and CDs. According to an AP/LifeGoesStrong.com survey:

- While a little over half of boomers are somewhat or very certain they'll be able to retire in comfort when the time comes, a full 44 percent have little or no confidence that they can swing it.

- Only 11 percent are strongly convinced they'll be well off when they retire.

- Nearly 6 in 10 said their nest eggs shrank during the recession, and 42 percent of those said they'd have to put off retirement because of it.

Excluding their homes, about a quarter of boomers say they have no retirement savings at all. Their empty bank accounts helped pull their median savings down to $40,000. Almost two-thirds expect Social Security to be the cornerstone of their retirement income.

On the other hand, while only about a third expect that they'll need to tone down their lifestyle after they quit working, many more underestimate exactly how expensive retirement can be, especially when living on a fixed income and dealing with cost-of-living and other increases. Yet about 25 percent of boomers are savvy enough to say they expect to never retire at all, and two-thirds of those still on the job said they planned to keep working after retirement. However, that may not be realistic, given the unstable and unpredictable unemployment rates.

Bottom line: We need to spend less and save more, and the next sections will show you how.

 ## BOOMERANG RETIREMENT FACTOIDS

The following can be downright daunting. So if you want to keep thinking everything is fine, skip this section. But unlike a movie, haunted house or other scary ride, closing your eyes won't make it go away:

- 36 percent of Americans say that they don't contribute anything at all to retirement savings.

- Most baby boomers do not have a traditional pension plan.

- Over 30 percent of U.S. investors currently in their sixties have more than 80 percent of their 401k invested in equities. So what happens if the stock market crashes again?

- 35 percent of Americans already over the age of 65 rely almost entirely on Social Security payments alone.

- 24 percent of U.S. workers admit that they have postponed their planned retirement age at least once during the past year.

- Three out of four Americans start claiming Social Security benefits the moment they are eligible at age 62. Most are doing this out of necessity. However, by claiming Social Security early they get locked in at a much lower amount than if they would have waited.

- In 1950, each retiree's Social Security benefit was paid for by 16 U.S. workers. In 2010, each retiree's Social Security benefit is paid for by approximately 3.3 U.S. workers. By 2025, there will be approximately 2 U.S. workers for each retiree. How can the system possibly continue to function properly with rapidly dropping numbers to support it?

- 40 percent of boomers plan to work "until they drop."

Summary

Stock market and home equity losses have emphasized the importance of safeguarding programs like Social Security and Medicare, the twin safety nets that could provide a higher portion of retirement support than many boomers originally bargained for. So while it's easier to pretend that everything is fine and go along with status quo, it's time to face some harsh realities. Solutions are difficult and challenging, but necessary if you want to retire and live comfortably.

STEVE SAYS

Banks are not your friends. They pay you "0 percent" on thousands of dollars that flow through your checking account and then charge you 6-30 percent if you want to borrow from them.

Part 4: The Wealth Death Spiral

Avoiding the Downward Trend

Even though the stock market crash of 2008 sounded a warning bell indicating the economy was nearing a precipice of disaster, problems had been brewing for decades. But, as with many things, it took a major event to get people to start connecting the dots and realize that the rules of wealth and security and a comfortable retirement had changed forever.

The "Death Spiral"

The combination of high and growing national debt, increased taxes, bankruptcies, returning inflation and municipal defaults can turn your planned retirement into a devastating wealth death spiral. For instance:

- If you were counting on stock market gains to grow your investment portfolio, the last 10 years returned literally nothing. This lost decade can't be recovered. It's gone.

- 401(k)s instantly became 201(k)s. Even though they recently recovered from 2008 levels, their return over the last decade is still about zero.

- Foreclosures and dropping home values have hit just about everyone in every market and still may not have reached rock bottom. The days of selling your house for big profits for your future retirement are over. You might even have to take a loss.

- Our national debt now tops $14.5 trillion and growing. We are paying a trillion dollars in interest a year and must borrow money from other countries just to keep our heads financially above water. Some politicians want to cut spending, while others are lobbying to increase taxes. Both national and state budgets are a mess, with countless fights breaking out in Congress, the Senate and within state legislatures. And there's no clear answer in sight.

- Bankruptcies are on the rise in our declining economy, and someone has to pay for the increased losses. This usually results in costs being passed on through increased interest rates and the lowered value of bonds, and can even affect a solvent person's ability to obtain a loan. As banks struggle to maintain reserves as loan losses mount, they tighten their standards, and their reluctance to risk their remaining assets can damage a struggling economy. Higher fees and rates will eliminate potential home-buyers from the system. This will put further downward pressure on home values and delay the recovery of this very large industry. As goes housing, goes the country; home values provide a good barometer of the overall economy. Credit is the jet fuel in a growing economy, but that is only needed when the consumer has confidence in their ability to get a job or maintain their current one.

- The return of inflation could make everything cost more. Printing more money would only exacerbate this problem.

- Municipal defaults not only impact bond investors, they directly affect services and local tax rates that ultimately take money away from citizens.

Life Insurance Can Be a Life Preserver

Some form of permanent life insurance has been around 1860. Ever since the tax laws were enacted by the 16th Amendment shortly after the turn of the 20th century, people have been using these policies to shelter their money. Whole life insurance was first and was followed by universal life insurance in the early 1980s. The equity index products of the 21st century provided an even more efficient way of protecting funds.

Traditionally, only people of wealth – or those who saved a fair chunk of change throughout their working lives – used life insurance policies for a decent rate of return and the tax shelters. But with tax laws changing and the debt that we have as a nation, many people are looking for tax shelters and a consistent rate of return.

For example, recently a client came to see me who was in his early 50s, owned a small business, and was married with children. During our first meeting, we discussed his assets, and he mentioned that in the early 1990s he had purchased a whole life policy that was now worth nearly $400,000 in cash value. When I asked why he deposited funds into a life insurance contract, he replied that his financial planner had advised him that this was what wealthy people did with their money, and where else could they earn 4 percent tax free and not have to worry about market conditions? Needless to say, he was even more enthusiastic about the EIUL, which allowed him to earn even more.

Life insurance has always offered a bit of a Catch-22 component. The traditional term policy only paid on death, which really didn't provide the deceased with much benefit! To get around this, a host of policies were created that allowed the owner to build up cash value and access the cash before they passed on.

STEVE SAYS

Common sense trumps get rich quick. Save early, save often, live within your means and if it sounds too good to be true, it probably is.

The new policies were great at first glance, but it quickly became apparent there was another problem – the returns were not particularly strong. Fixed return products would return growth at a 2-4 percent rate.

The equity indexed life insurance policy is designed to resolve this issue. The policy has a traditional cash account like a universal policy. The difference is that the growth mechanism is pegged to an equity index that tracks the stock market. Depending on the policy, the growth comes with a double cap. On one hand, it caps the potential growth each year to a maximum of say 12 percent, but also caps the potential loss to zero percent. This gives you an assurance of growth with little or no risk, making it extremely profitable in most situations.

Summary

As insurmountable as many of the wealth-destroying factors seem, you can minimize their harm and create a secure retirement money wave. This strategy will enable you to generate a tax-free, positive return on your investment and build a secure financial future. The rest of this book will lay out this plan in detail and teach you the new rules of money.

Part 5: Growing and Protecting Your Assets

The 7 Rules for Wealth

Like any worthwhile effort, saving money and building wealth are never easy, and require discipline, persistence and patience. However, these seven rules can provide a blueprint towards creating retirement security.

Rule 1: Save More

Somewhere along the line, most Americans lost sight of this first, and most important, rule. Their parents or grandparents learned how to save during the Great Depression of the 1930s, when many people lost their life savings and jobs, and there was very little to live on. Back then, you made do with what you had and put a little aside for the future, in case things got even worse. If you didn't have the money for it, you couldn't buy it. It was that simple.

But when prosperity returned in the 1950s, the parents of the baby boom generation wanted to give their children all the material things they'd lacked, and oops, forgot to mention that it was probably a good idea to save a percentage of what they made. Or maybe they did try to teach their children, and their kids weren't listening – who wants to put money away into something as boring and seemingly far away as retirement, when you can go someplace fun or buy a cool new gadget? So, along with the increasingly easy-to-get and expanding credit, a collapsing housing market and the other factors discussed earlier, the current financial crisis was born. By then, the damage was done and many Americans had all the big-screen TVs, nice cars and fancy vacations their straining finances could handle, along with tremendous debt.

This "live for today and let tomorrow take care of itself" mentality has already begun to catch up with some who have been thrown into retirement early. They expected to work another few years and build up their retirement accounts, along with paying off the mortgage and any debt. But the recession took their job and drained their finances, and where are they now?

But it's never too late to start, although the earlier you begin to save, the better. The key thing to remember is to save money and put it away. It provides peace of mind, comfort and security. It's also good for your health because financial stress and worrying about debt can contribute to all kinds of physical ailments.

Rule 2: Live on at Least 15 Percent Less Than You Earn

Successful people learn to live within their means. And most of the time it comes down to plain old discipline. Certain modifications can be practically painless. For example, review your deductibles on car, health and homeowner's insurance. By raising them, you can save 15 percent or less; simply put that money away each month into a retirement account. There are also other ways to economize, but the bottom line is when you do get extra money, save it rather than spend it.

By cutting down here and there (even if it's difficult at times), teach yourself how to learn to live on 15-20 percent less than you make. Many people think that this only means cutting back on vacations, eating out and trips to the store. Most Americans could very easily increase their savings rates even more if they just understood a few key things that banks and insurance companies don't want you to know. Raising deductibles on their car, home or health insurance can save hundreds or even thousands of dollars each year. Americans want wealth without sacrifice, which is why the latter strategies are so powerful. If you understand and implement them, you may not have to sacrifice nearly as much.

Consider the millionaires in this country. Most live in average homes and make decent, not fantastic, salaries. They just know where every penny goes and use it wisely. They manage to have a great lifestyle and nice things, but you can't even tell they're millionaires! The sad truth is that only about 7 percent of the American population will ever achieve that type of financial security.

Rule 3: Practice Discipline in Putting Money Away for Retirement

It's called "pay yourself first." I have money every month that goes into my retirement account. I don't see it. I don't touch it. I don't have to write a check. I don't even think about it. It's done automatically. Bottom line: If it's not there, you don't spend it.

When you do that, you learn to live within your means. So, if you want to save more, then pay yourself more first. If you're saving 5 percent now, ramp it up to 10-15 percent.

If you find that you absolutely cannot do this, then figure out how to bring more revenue into your household. I recently had a client who'd racked up $70,000 in credit card debt. Although he had a great job and worked over 50 hours a week, his wife had a part-time business that was more like a hobby, and was in fact costing them money.

The solution was obvious, although painful, especially for the wife. She needed to get rid of the dead-weight business and find a job that made money so they could begin to pay down the debt while saving for the future.

STEVE SAYS

Work hard and smart – most successful people take whatever time is needed to do the job well. Find something that you love so it won't feel like a chore.

Try to run your finances as though they're a business. If things are upside-down and you have more bills than income, it's time to bring in more revenue. This could be in a form of a part-time job or setting up a tight budget that involves cutting expenses and allowing X amount of dollars for food, clothing and other essentials that you can control, such as the phone bill and TV/Internet access. It can be painful, yes, but necessary.

Consistently put those savings into an account that is secure and difficult to withdraw from. That way, if you're tempted by a new jet-ski, or any other passing fancy, you'll think twice before you raid your retirement fund, particularly if it involves penalties.

Also consider how the money is growing and compounding as it sits in that account. The compounding effect of money is one of the most powerful factors in accumulating wealth, whether you're 22, 52, or 72. You can never turn back the clock, and if you take the money out, you remove all past and future benefits. On the hand, if you keep putting in money in, you're giving yourself time to live comfortably in the future. Get started here and now, and that leverage of time will do great things for you down the road.

Rule 4: Manage Your Debt

This recession has been beneficial in one way. As the government ramps up billions of dollars of debt a day, personal debt is winding down. With millions of Americans out of work – or newly returning to work, even – they have become more aware of where their dollars are going and are paying down their debt instead of adding to it. And the banks have helped somewhat; they've cut down or eliminated the barrage of credit card offers. They've also made it difficult for people with financial problems or excessive debt to obtain credit and now require a decent credit score and proof of income.

But credit cards are only part of the problem. Other types of debt can also create difficulties. For example, I used to go out and buy the latest and flashiest model car and never bothered to pay off the other two or three I had. I told myself I could always trade them in.

But then I started understanding the rules of money. I used to justify it as, "Hey honey, that car is red and shiny and it's only going to cost us $399 a month." Then I began to realize it wasn't just $399 a month but $20,000, $30,000 or $40,000 for the cost of a car that was sticker-priced at approximately 50 percent of the total loan, and sometimes even more than that.

Consider the opportunities lost. That money that could have been sitting in a retirement account, earning interest for you instead of being paid to a bank. That's what was so destructive to me and a lot of other people. So when I drive down the road with my paid-off and practical Honda Accord and see the millionaire wannabes in their tricked-out Navigators and Mercedes, I have to chuckle. I am saving tens of thousands of dollars or whatever that new car cost, plus interest. Not only that, but it's sitting in my account earning 8 percent and adding as much as $250,000 to my retirement fund. Of course, I still buy cars. Not as often though, and before I purchase, I always think about the long-term opportunity loss from mismanaged debt.

It can be the same situation with buying homes. For years people have been told to refinance their homes and mortgages. Not only do they get a lower rate, but they might also get some equity to pay off debt or buy even more stuff. But refinancing can extend the life of your mortgage and add to your total overall debt. While most people don't pay off their mortgages entirely during their lifetimes, it's still possible to get close and add equity to your retirement.

For example, say you get a 5 percent 30-year mortgage on a home worth $250,000. You end up paying somewhere between $200,000-$250,000 in interest. That's right – almost double the price of the home. And that's if you never refinance it again. Consider what that interest could have done had it been sitting in your retirement account.

Of course you get a tax deduction. And you need a place to live. But by refinancing and spending the equity, you may have cheated yourself out of a major retirement savings opportunity.

So if you haven't done so already, stop thinking with your emotions, and carefully evaluate those major purchases that can be so destructive to your finances over the long haul. Make sure you can afford it, pay the bills and still put money away.

Rule 5: Know the Difference Between Good and Bad Debt

Good debt will enhance or improve your financial future and position in life. It's typically at a lower interest rate and may have a tax or other benefit. Bad debt will take away from your opportunity to gain financial security.

There are several examples of good debt. As mentioned earlier, the wise choice of a mortgage is not only a tax deduction but provides a place to live. Another example is a business loan. As a business owner, you might have the potential to land a new contract or create a needed product that may require some cash to expand operations. Without the infusion of money, you might lack the resources to apply for the contract or bring in the revenue. Education is another example of a good loan, as long the person utilizes the degree and/or training.

Under certain circumstances, even credit cards represent good debt. When I first started out, I couldn't get a business loan, so I had to put some costs on a credit card. But rather than using it to live beyond my means, I saw it as financial tool and paid it off quickly, keeping in mind the high, cumulative interest rates.

In general, however, credit cards are the epitome of bad debt. Unfortunately, for many – in the past, myself included – they become a lifestyle and an excuse to make excessive purchases you might not otherwise be able to afford. For example, a married couple recently came into my office for a financial consultation. They were putting $1200 a month towards credit card payments and only $500 a month into their 401(k). Who is getting rich in this scenario? Of course, it's the banks.

The bottom line is, get rid of bad debt. The more it accumulates, the less chance you have of getting ahead. And without bad debt, if you're living within your means, you can still take trips, buy cars and accumulate wealth at the same time.

For a long time, Americans failed to understand the concept of bad debt, but they're starting to get the idea. Now we need to get the government in Washington, DC to understand this!

Rule 6: Reduce Your Tax Liabilities – Tax Deferred Is Not Tax Free

During their lifetimes, the average American will pay about 31-33 percent of every dollar they ever make towards some kind of tax. And approximately another 30 percent will go to pay interest on loans. That's a total of 60+ percent going to taxes and interest! No wonder it's hard to have a decent lifestyle and put away money.

However, you can do certain things to lower taxes. For example, if you have a 401(k), match whatever percentage your employer contributes. Not only is this free money, but also your employer is basically paying future taxes on your retirement. Also, by funding that money into that account, you lower your adjusted gross income and get to keep more of what you make right now. Another effective way to lower your tax bill is through the write-off on your mortgage. Many so-called financial experts will tell you to pay off your mortgage as soon as possible and then start saving. With fewer and fewer tax breaks and with low interest rates on mortgages, this may not be in your best interest.

There are many other ways to reduce taxes, which is why it's important to find a good CPA. But with regards to retirement savings, other questions still remain: Is there any way to control paying excessive taxes in the future? How can you tell what the rates will be?

As mentioned in Part 2, when 401(k)s and IRAs were created in the late 1970s, it was based on the idea that when you retired, you would be in a lower tax bracket. This could still be technically true, because back then tax rates under Jimmy Carter maxed out at 70 percent.

But tax rates started to drop under Ronald Reagan and have continued to do so. Now the highest marginal bracket currently is 35 percent. It's expected to go back up to 39.5 percent in 2013. And Social Security is also now a taxable event, a change from when 401(k)s and IRAs were created. As of this writing, if you make over $32,000 a year, up to 50 percent of your Social Security is included as taxable income. If that figure is over $44,000 a year, it's up to 85 percent.

Say that you retire and start taking distributions from your 401(k)s, IRAs, Thrift Saving Plans or other deferred savings plan. It all comes out as taxable income. And now half or 85 percent of your Social Security is taxable income. Your pension, if you have one, is also taxable.

But what happens if your tax rate goes up in the future instead of getting lower, or even staying the same? What happens if now you're in an even higher tax bracket, say up

STEVE SAYS

Education, financial and otherwise, is a lifelong process. The economy, financial strategies, taxes and financial products constantly change. You are never too young to start learning and never too old to stop!

to 40 percent, instead of that 25 percent marginal bracket you were in while working? And while people say that increasing taxes may only include the high-income earners, you too could become a victim of "bracket creep," thanks to the cumulative income resulting from your pension, investments and Social Security, not mention reduced deductions (even adult children who live at home eventually usually move out).

Therefore, tax deferred is not always tax free. Not even close. And given the likelihood that taxes will continue to increase, deferring to a future time would probably be unwise. I'd rather pay now and take all the deductions that I can. Failure to factor in what taxes are now and/or what they will be in the future will make it very difficult to accumulate, maintain and grow your retirement assets.

Rule 7: Put Your Money in Life Insurance and Other Secure Investments

A handful of safe and secure products allow you to put your money into them and still have tax-free access to it in the future. One of the most secure places for funds is life insurance, which has been around even before the creation of the US income tax in 1913.

 ## A LIFE INSURANCE TAX PRIMER

Certain types of life insurance have tax benefits. They include:

* Whole life insurance—Created in 1860, it is still offered by a handful of

companies. Returns are typically around 4 percent; most people who fund these accounts do so for tax-free access while they're living. The remainder goes to the heirs tax-free.

- Universal life insurance – Invented by the E.F. Hutton Company in 1980, it combines many of the same tax benefits with a higher percentage of growth.

- Variable Universal Life – This life contract typically has stocks and mutual funds as the growth mechanism. It worked well when the stock market was consistent but not during volatile times.

- Equity indexed universal – A more recent evolution of universal life insurance, this equity index product can be linked to stock indices such as the S&P 500, NASDAQ or the DOW. They generally have a 0-2 percent floor that protects your accounts and investments and a cap of 10-17 percent that allows your money to increase along with the stock market.

Some equity index universal insurance products have a floor of 0 and a cap of 15 percent. If you purchased the policy on May 15, 2011, the S&P would be tracked between then and the following year (May15, 2012) and whatever it did up until the highest cap is your rate of return and what's credited to your account.

A word of warning - insurance policies have additional costs. Along with a sales charge and maintenance fees, there's the cost of the death benefit which is based on your age, sex and general health as well as how much cash you're putting into the policy. Therefore, the key is a properly planned contract designed to get minimum insurance and maximum cash into the policy.

Summary

The way to access the funds in your EIUL is to borrow them out. When you borrow money against the policy, it comes out tax free. The loan never exceeds your maximum benefit. The insurance company takes the money out of their general reserves, loans it to you and then upon death, pays itself back.

Taxes? No problem!

Part 6: The Retirement Money Wave Strategy

Putting It All Together

The world we live in now is far different than what most people planned and worked for. The reality is, your future is at risk. Everything you have saved and invested may be worth much less than expected, and what you do own could be taxed at rates that could reduce your wealth by 50 percent or more.

So far we've discussed how the declining economy, policy makers and aging boomers have jeopardized your dream of retiring comfortably. But there's still time to not only protect your retirement savings, but create your own personal retirement money wave. The salvation comes in the forms of IRS Code Sections 7702 and 72(e), which, although they apply to all policies, helped encourage the creation of universal life insurance, the equity indexed universal life insurance (EIUL) policies discussed earlier. This section will tell you how you can use this insurance to create a tax-free income stream for retirement.

Tax Free Trumps Taxed and Tax Deferred

Because tax laws are constantly changing and increases may be in the offing, it is more important than ever to consider the impact on taxable vs. tax- free retirement savings. As discussed earlier, tax-deferred does not necessarily lower the amount of taxes you pay. And every dollar you pay in taxes from that tax-deferred account is one less that you have for retirement.

For example, say you have a $100,000 investment. Using a 36 percent combined federal and state tax bracket, $100,000 earning 6 percent for 25 years in a taxed growth investment would become $256,517. The same amount invested in a tax-free investment (such as an EIUL) would become $429,187. This comparison assumes no withdrawals would be made. As Figure 6.1 shows, a tax-free investment creates an additional $172,670 of tax-free income.

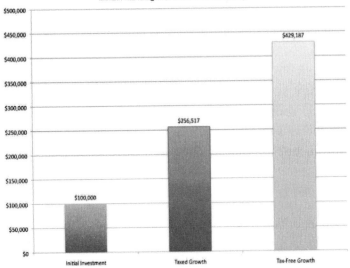

Figure 6.1. *Taxed vs. Tax-Free Growth of $100,000 Investment*

In short, if you want to maximize your retirement savings you'll need to focus on minimizing your taxes on investment results. This is where the EUIL pays off in spades.

The 411 on EIULs

Not only does an EIUL policy provide numerous benefits while you're living, but also to your family upon death. Additionally, it offers flexible premiums and funding, which means you can deposit money in smaller amounts on a monthly basis. You can start with a lower amount, and add more funds over the years as your income rises.

Each EIUL has a minimum payment based on the age, sex, and initial death benefit. The suggested funding amount, or target premium is a total annual sum that can be funded monthly, quarterly, semi-annually or annually. Each policy also has a maximum annual amount or modified endowment contract (MEC) guideline, which is solely based on IRS regulations regarding age, sex, health and death benefits.

While each EIUL has a floor and a ceiling, it also tracks a stock index, such as the S&P 500, NASDAQ, or Dow Jones. While the money's not actually in the stock market, it simply follows its trends while maintaining a minimum and maximum rate of return, such as a floor of 0 and a cap of 15 percent.

Unlike the highly volatile stock market, the money in the accumulation account remains stable. For example, when the stock market lost 46 percent of its value from 2000-02, money in these policies would have remained the same. So if it had a floor of 0, you basically lost nothing instead of 46 percent. On the other side of the equation, had the opposite been true, you would have earned the cap of whatever was in your EIUL policy contract (say, 15 percent) rather than the full 46 percent. In return for not getting any of the downside of the market, you do give up some of the upside. However, as nice as it is to see huge gains, it's far more important to avoid double-digit losses.

Two other key features of the EIUL are lock in and reset, which help these products make money even in a volatile market. With lock in, the gains or the "0" are credited to your account on the anniversary date of your purchase of the policy. Each year the gains are different. Reset means that the next year tracks the point that the index was on that last day of the previous year. The resulting effect of this is if you have a floor of "0" and a top cap of 12-15 percent, your accumulation account "goes up and sideways" not "up and down," like most accounts with stocks or mutual funds. So your money is "linked to" the stock market, as opposed to being directly in it!

For example, say that Bob's policy was approved on May 1, 2009. His EUIL would track an index such as the S & P 500 for 365 days. If the index went up by 10 percent and he was in the annual point to point, with a floor of 0 and a cap of 15 percent, his account would be credited 10 percent and those funds would lock in automatically to his account. If the markets had been negative, then he would have locked in a 0, meaning he would have neither made nor lost anything. The start of Year 2 on the policy, the index would start from the ending point of the previous year; in Bob's case, April 30, 2010? Combined with the floor and the cap, they allow for growth during even these turbulent times.

Along with a tax-free death benefit to the heirs, another benefit is tax-free access to the gains while living. However, you will need to comply with certain rules pertaining to the EIULs. Say a 40-year-old male puts $800 per month for five years into an EIUL instead of a 401(k) account, but then he stops depositing money into it. As long as he begins to contribute again after a period of time, the policy should be fine. But if he has to or wants to cease putting money in altogether, then he will need to lower the death benefit, also known as the face amount.

Reviewing the account's performance on an annual basis is always recommended. This allows for changes to funding and, if needed, revisions to the size of the policy. Owners will need to keep enough funds in the policy to make sure it stays in force.

Another potential problem is that not all policies are created equal. Some are very good, but others are outdated and provide far fewer benefits and returns. For example, variable universal life (VUL) policies were popular in the 1990s and early 2000s when the stock market was more stable. VULs had the tax benefits of a permanent policy, but typically included stocks and/or mutual funds as the growth mechanism. This only works well when the market is predicable, and when it crashed, people lost money in their VULs.

How EIULS Stack Up

In equity indexed policies, the performance of the cash value depends on what the market is doing. However, equity indexed policies also have "floors" and "ceilings" built in so that they will never perform worse than a certain percent, nor will they exceed a certain percent since it's capped at the ceiling. Figure 6.2 illustrates how the floor and ceiling come into play in earning cash returns.

STEVE SAYS

While it's been said that you learn more from your mistakes then from your successes it's far more profitable to learn from the mistakes of others.

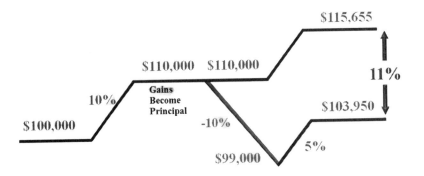

Figure 6.2. Floor and Ceiling Variables in the EIUL

Features and advantages

- No age or income restrictions

- Guaranteed safety, exceptional liquidity

- Outstanding tax-free rates of return

- Based on IRS Code Sections 7702 and 72(e)

The accumulation of cash inside the insurance contract is tax advantaged. Not only can the cash value accumulate tax free, but it can also be accessed tax free. Hence, the beauty and magic of the EIUL; it is a unique vehicle that allows for tax-free account value accumulation, permits you to access your money tax free, and, when you die, blossoms in value and transfers income tax free!

Equity indexed life insurance offers the upside potential of stock market performance and a guard against downside risk with a guaranteed minimum interest rate (floor). It combines most of the features, benefits and security of traditional life insurance with the potential to earn interest based on the upward movement of an equity index. Instead of the insurer declaring a specific interest rate or dividend as with traditional life insurance, interest earnings are credited based on the increases in value of a specific equity index.

The Standard & Poor 500 composite stock price index (excluding dividends) is currently the most commonly used index for EIULs. Credited interest is linked to increases in the S&P 500 index without the downside risks associated with investing directly in the stock market. And because EIULs are permanent life insurance plans, they provide additional advantages and financial stability through:

- A guaranteed minimum interest rate
- Tax-deferred interest accumulation
- Access to cash value through withdrawal and loan provisions
- Distributions are not included in income calculations for Social Security taxation
- Principal guarantees
- Annual lock-in of index gains, annual reset of index
- Minimum rate of return combined with maximum cap on gains
- Tax-free distributions

In addition, the equity indexed link in EIUL products offer:

- Equity index-linked returns with the potential to beat inflation

- Protection in the contract against downside market risk

How It Works

There are three components to a life insurance policy:

- The owner

- The insured

- The beneficiary

Each of these components can be held by different people. You do not have to be the insured to be the owner of the policy. Many of our clients are not the insured, but own and control the cash distributions of the equity index life contract.

A licensed insurance professional such as an insurance agent or financial advisor must be used to purchase these products. Be careful to choose a professional who knows how to properly design the EIUL to maximize growth and minimize costs.

To obtain a policy:

1. Applicant identifies goals, objectives and resources

2. Application is completed and submitted

3. Funding method is determined (over a period of time, or as lump sum, such as over 5 years)

4. Insurance company reviews application

5. Medical exam (some, but not all, medical conditions are accepted)

6. Contract is approved and funded

7. The contract stipulates both a floor (usually about 0-2 percent) and a ceiling (12-15 percent). If the pegged index has a negative return, no loss is incurred. Each year gains are captured and become principal.

Getting an EIUL

How and where can you find the best EIUL to meet your needs? A financial professional licensed to sell life insurance is a good source. Along with a working knowledge of the EIULs, they should be able to answer questions concerning the policy, as well as funding and loan options. The process of getting an EIUL can be broken down into the following steps:

Step 1. Look over the field. There are many EIULs to choose from. First, you'll want to make sure it's a solid company with strong financials that has been around for a long time. Then, you'll need to determine the EIUL's floor and cap; these were previously discussed on page 86. Finally, you'll need to find out the provisions of the EIUL – how much it costs to borrow from it and what happens to the interest in the remaining balance, as well as any money you are already putting into it. You'll also need to clarify whether it includes a wash, or zero cost, loan. With these types of loans, if a client needs $100,000 from their policy, the insurance company will loan it to the client from their cash reserves and charge them, for example, 6 percent. Since the clients $100,000 is sitting safely in their policy, the insurance company will "credit" them 6 percent. So, while they were being charged $6,000 for the money they borrowed, they also earned $6,000 on their account. The net effect is no cost to use the money, thus making it a "wash."

Step 2. Determine what monies you're going to use to fund the policy. Will they come from funds that may have gone into a 401(k), IRA, TSP, savings or other account?

An option may be to max fund a policy; that is, put in the maximum amount allowed. Say you come into a large sum of cash, either from selling something or an inheritance. Several years ago I had a 40-year-old male client who sold a home at a $200,000 profit and decided to max fund an EIUL. Using the IRS guidelines and with a $1.2 million policy, the insurance company stated that the maximum allowable deposit would be $51,000 per year for four years. After that, the client could not deposit any additional funds until after the eleventh year; if he did, all of the gains would become taxable. However, he can deposit money during the twelfth year and beyond, if he wishes.

Step 3. Have a professional help you build a policy that will help you maximize your money. This means striking a fine balance. If the policy is too large, the COI will eat away at your cash and minimize your growth. Nor can it be too small; otherwise, it may fail to meet the IRS modified endowment contract (MEC) funding guidelines.

Step 4. Apply for the life insurance policy. Because the EIUL is a life insurance policy, you will need to take and pass a physical. After the agent or advisor takes your application, an independent contractor will be hired by the insurance company to come to your home to perform the examination, typically at no cost. The average policy normally requires just a basic check of your overall health, perhaps a review of prior medical records and a phone interview. If a large death benefit is involved, you may need to have a more intensive exam at a hospital.

If someone has medical issues, a spouse may be used as the insured. In one case, the husband was recovering from cancer, but the wife was healthy. The wife can be the insured, and both he and the wife can be owners of the policy.

Step 5. Underwriting. Review panels at the life insurance company will look over all the data and approve as is, decline for health issues, request more information, rate the policy and/or offer a reduced death benefit. Rating involves how much you pay for premiums based upon your general health. Say a 50-year-old male applies for preferred non-tobacco on a $500,000 policy, and after the medical exam and underwriting, the insurance company offers a standard non-tobacco rating. This raises the COI and takes away from the growth in the accumulation account. A good strategy might be to lower the death benefit slightly to $475,000, keeping the COI at the desired level.

Step 6. Delivery. Once the policy has been approved, the agent sets up a time to review and deliver the policy. Once you have signed it and deposited the funds, it is in force.

Step 7. Annual Statements. When you receive your annual statement, sit down with your financial advisor and review the account. Things to consider include market performance and whether you need to make funding adjustments or make a change in beneficiaries.

Funding the Life Insurance Contract

We have discussed redirecting funds from 401(k)s, savings, home equity or other investments into the life insurance contract. You can also invest any extra cash, and regardless of the amount, it can be redirected and funded into the EIUL.

 ## CASE STUDY: WILLIAM SMITH

William Smith (not his real name) is 33 years old, married with two children and owns his own business. Even though he already had $16,500 in his 401(k), he decided to stop funding the 401(k) and redirect the monies into the EIUL.

If he funds the EIUL until age 65 and starts taking money out then, he should be able to withdraw over $300,000 a year tax free as long as his account remains unchanged, and as long as the S&P continues with the same trends as it has over the past 40 years (taking into consideration the fluctuation in the market). If he decides to quit funding it earlier, say at age 50, he would get about $176,000 a year. Again, these are based on what the product would do with the floor and the cap as they currently stand. Companies that offer these products can reduce the caps, meaning a company with a 14 percent cap could reduce it to 13 percent or even lower in the future. Competition from other companies, market conditions and contract language can also result in changes.

William purchased a $2 million life insurance policy. Along with being based on the IRS formula, this figure allowed William to maximize his EIUL. Other considerations included his age, sex, health and the amount of money he could afford to fund into the account.

William also has a couple of choices as to how he could put money into the policy. He could max fund it; that is, put in as much as $57,000 a year for four years. The $57,000 is the modified endowment contract (MEC) limit set by the IRS, so he could put in a total of about $220,000 in four years, but then could not contribute another penny until the start of the 12th year, at which time he could go back and make annual payments of $16,500 for the rest of his life if he so desired. Or he could target fund the EIUL by simply putting in $16,500 every year.

Why put all that money in at once? Well, compounding growth is simple math. The quicker you can get money into an account, the more it's going to grow and compound. He can also contribute on a monthly, quarterly, semiannually or annual basis, or skip a year or two if he needs to. He's not obligated. It's not a contract. He doesn't have to fund it for the rest of his life, but if he chooses to skip too many years, it may make sense to reduce the death benefit to maximize the cash already deposited into the account.

William has all his bases covered. Should he die at a younger than expected age, then the $2 million policy will help take care of his wife and children.

Figure 6.3 charts the comparison between the S&P index and an equity index insurance contract over a period of 11 years. As you can see, the S&P yielded an account balance of $90,702, while the EIUL produced over twice as much, some $200,835. The life insurance never lost principal, even in the years that the S&P had negative returns. And although the high return years are capped, the average rate of return (ROR) for the EIUL remains significantly higher.

Comparison Between the S&P Index and the Equity Index Universal Life Contract for 11 years				
Year	Historical Return of S&P 500	$100,000 Basis	Index Universal Life Policy	$100,000 Basis
2000	19.50%	$119,500	15.00%	$115,000
2001	-10.14%	$107,383	0.00%	$115,000
2002	-13.04%	$93,380	0.00%	$115,000
2003	-23.37%	$71,557	0.00%	$115,000
2004	26.38%	$90,434	15.00%	$132,250
2005	8.99%	$98,564	8.99%	$144,139
2006	3.00%	$101,521	3.00%	$148,463
2007	13.62%	$115,348	13.62%	$168,684
2008	3.53%	$119,420	3.53%	$174,639
2009	-38.50%	$73,443	0.00%	$174,639
2010	23.50%	$90,702	15.00%	$200,835
Acct Balance		90,702		$200,835
Avg ROR	-0.88%		6.54%	
A cap of 15% and a floor of 0% using an annual point to point option				

Figure 6.3. Comparison Between S&P Index and Equity Index Insurance Contract

Funding through Equity Harvesting

Sometimes you can build more wealth by borrowing money against your home or another asset and only paying down some of the debt versus aggressively using all the funds and becoming debt-free. If you can manage it financially, an equity harvesting strategy that involves putting the money in an EIUL will help you grow the maximum amount of wealth possible.

Below are some advantages of harvesting equity:

- You can borrow money with a low interest rate and reinvest the proceeds in a policy that earns a higher rate of return.

- You can write off the interest on part of or the entire loan.

- You are investing in a tax-favorable environment where the money can grow tax-free and can come out tax-free in retirement.

From a financial standpoint and when done properly, equity harvesting, borrowing money to reposition it in a tax-favorable manner and being able to write off the interest on the borrowed funds, is a great strategy. Even if you cannot write off the interest, equity harvesting can be a terrific wealth building tool.

STEVE SAYS

It may not always make sense to pay off your home. In creating wealth and compounding growth, "today" is the most important day. Taking money that could be accumulating in a high-interest earning account is more profitable than paying off a low-interest mortgage that also provides a tax break.

CASE STUDY: SUZY JONES

Suzy Jones (not her real name) was a 42-year-old business owner who took out a $170,000 home equity line of credit to put into a $1 million EIUL. After following the IRS guidelines that determine how much cash she could invest (based on age, sex, health including smoker/ nonsmoker and amount available), she decided to pay the maximum amount, $38,000, annually over five years. She could have deposited a much smaller amount monthly or annually if she wanted, but she knew that compounding works best by placing the most money in as quickly as possible. After that, the EIUL was paid in full; not another penny went into the account. Again, this was based on IRS codes 7702 and 72e.

If the S&P 500 performs over the next 50 years as it has in the past, when she retires at age 65 she'll be able to take out about $75,000 a year over the next 30 years and even longer, if need be. Yet she put in only $170,000. Even if she takes out two-thirds of that $1 million policy plus its earnings, upon her death, the family would still get what's left; in this example, after 30 years of retirement, some $852,000.

But for now, Suzy continues working. She can use the money to help her kids through college, for her business or to buy a new minivan. She can take the money out of the account, even if she's not yet 59 ½. It doesn't matter. It's not an IRA or 401(k). She can put it back or not. Either way, she avoids paying taxes on the money. How cool is that?

How to Generate Your Tax-Free Retirement Money Wave

After you have funded and watched your insurance contract grow, you can start pulling out funds tax-free by using a provision in the agreement that treats those disbursements as loans. The interest charge is often balanced out by the income that would have been earned. Because of various contingencies discussed in this and earlier sections, this return of money is neither reported on IRS form 1090 nor does it count towards Social Security payment eligibility. It also would not be shown as an asset on college loan applications.

Summary

Rather than being the enclave of the very wealthy, the equity index life insurance contract has become a safe haven for many people, regardless of income. With the tax laws changing and the increasing national debt, people are looking for tax shelters and a consistent rate of return.

EIULs offer a security net and solid ROR. They also utilize growth compounding and, as such, can be far more profitable than only putting your money in the stock market, a 401(k) or other investment. Best of all, you don't pay taxes when you take money out nor do your heirs upon receiving the death benefit.

However, you'll need to be willing to factor in the cost of insurance (COI), which can include higher premiums for illnesses. In most cases, if you work with a professional, the redirection of underperforming assets or the recapturing of interest on credit cards or loans will have little or no effect on your lifestyle, yet it will create financial security. As long as you fund it according to the IRS rules, all gains come out tax-free. Considering the trillions of dollars of government debt, it makes sense to have a portion of your assets accessible to you and tax-free.

PART 7: FUNDING YOUR PERSONAL PENSION PLAN

EIULs, EIAS and Your Assets

Over the past decade, millions of Americans have had their retirement accounts devastated by the so-called "New Economy." This means that, unlike recessions of the past, which lasted 12 months and occurred between 3–5 years of growth, there are more dramatic downturns followed by longer periods in which stocks return to their original levels. Trillions of dollars in federal, state, and local government debt, the declining housing market, and other factors are causing the economy and the markets to perform more like they did during the Great Depression in the U.S or more recently, in Japan, as discussed in Part 3.

If you plan on relying on Social Security and existing retirement savings to provide financial security, you may discover that you will have to make severe, cost-cutting lifestyle changes. One way to avoid this is to turn your existing 401(k), IRA and/or thrift savings plan (TSP) into a personal pension plan. You can also use funds from other sources as well.

The Importance of Having an Annuity

In the introduction to this book, we talked about the three "buckets" of money:

- Short term – Cash, checking account or a money market at your local bank. These accounts are more about liquidity and safety than the rate of return.

- Intermediate term – This could be a certificate of deposit (CD) or a fixed annuity. These products should earn 2-5 percent for 2-5 years.

- Long term – These are the Equity Indexed Universal Life policies (EIULs) or Equity Indexed Annuities (EIAs) discussed in this chapter.

401(k)s, IRAs, TSPs and SEP IRAs were, by their very nature, supposed to provide an income stream throughout a person's "golden years." Unfortunately, many people have discovered that while saving strategies worked well to build the accounts, they hardly ensured that the owner would have a guaranteed paycheck for life.

The only way to create a reliable income stream is through an annuity, a fixed sum of money paid out each year, typically for life. Sources such as the General Accounting Office (GAO), Wharton School of Business and *Smart Money*

Magazine have recently recommended that retirees have at least some annuities in their assets.

With an annuity, the insurance company basically "insures" your retirement account. They can pay you for the rest of your life, depending on the product you choose, the company itself, the amount deposited, years of deferment, rate of return and when you decide to start drawing a check. Many products allow you the option of ensuring that your spouse will continue receiving those checks in the event of your death. And, like most financial products, there are plenty to choose from.

Equity Indexed Annuities (EIAs)

An EIA, also known as an index annuity, is a type of tax-deferred annuity whose credited interest is linked to an equity index. EIAs have been around for decades in one form or another. In the past, poor rates of return and long surrender fees gave many a bad name. However, they have recently become popular when rolling over qualified assets, particularly as the stock market has become more unstable and unpredictable.

EIAs range from short-term products to those that can last a lifetime. EIAs have no loads (commissions or sales charges), fees or other expenses but they do have surrender fees if the owner takes out more than the contracted amount per year or walks away before all fees phase out.

Many EIAs have 2 -10 years worth of surrender fees, and most will allow the owner to withdraw up to 10 percent per year starting in the second year. If you take out more than that, penalties might apply.

In most EIAs, the client will have to take out the funds in an income stream in order to receive the fixed rate of return. And having a "predictable" rate of return in your account provides peace of mind, especially as you get close to retirement.

For example, at age 61, Sam rolled his old $100,000 IRA into an EIA. A little more than a year later, at age 62, Sam was able to take out up to $10,000 without any surrender charges. However, if something did go wrong and were he to immediately need all his funds, he would lose his bonus and 10 percent of the $100,000. However, Sam is planning on working until age 66 and has set up a "rainy day fund", so he's comfortable with EIA setup. This product provides him peace of mind and his $100,000 is protected from stock market corrections.

Looking at it another way, say you lose 50 percent of your 401(k) in a year, and it drops from $600,000 to $300,000. While it might be disconcerting to be penalized should you roll it into an EIA and then unexpectedly have take out the money, you would likely lose a lot more in an unstable stock market. $30,000 in surrender fees is a lot less than $300,000!

Some EIAs also offer an income rider that allows for a fixed rate of return for the years the money sits in deferment. This means the client knows exactly what they will have in their account each year. Percentages generally vary from [please provide numbers].

Spouses usually inherit the EIA upon the death of the owner. If both husband and wife have died, then the heirs receive the account balance in one payment, or in some cases over a period of years.

EIULS VS EIAS

EIAs and EIULs are similar in many ways:

- Are contracts with an insurance or annuity company

- Can't lose money

- Have a floor which is normally "0"

- Are linked to an index like the S&P 500, NASDAQ, DOW or others

- Have lock in and reset features

- Have surrender charges that vary in length and percentage

Unlike EIULS, however, EIAs do not have loads, fees or expenses.

Summary

EUILs have many benefits, especially for boomers approaching retirement. While you may have to modify and reduce your lifestyle somewhat to fund an EIUL, you will find that the long-term payout will help provide financial security for you and your family.

EIAs are great products to "rollover" an IRA, 401(k), TSP and others because it can help you create your own private pension plan. This can mean a paycheck for life and with some indexed annuities, possibly even a pay raise for life.

Part 8: Create Your Legacy

Transferring Your Wealth to the Next Generation

With trillions of dollars of government debt at the federal, state and local levels, tax rates will likely be rising for everyone. And while only the very wealthy may have to pay estate taxes, nearly all families must deal with income taxes on qualified accounts. These include inherited retirement accounts such as 401(k)s, IRAS, TSPS, SEP IRAS and others left behind by family and loved ones.

EIUL Life Insurance Beneficiaries and Benefits

A permanent life insurance policy to help pay income and/ or estate taxes will help ensure asset transfer from one generation to the next. To take a hypothetical example, say Robert's father had accumulated $500,000 in his 401(k), and now both of his parents have passed away. With Robert as the sole beneficiary and with no estate taxes due under the current laws, most people would think that Robert just had a windfall of a half million dollars. However, strings are attached – and they can cut pretty deeply. Since this is a 401(k), no taxes have been paid, and Uncle Sam will want his portion as soon as Robert takes out the cash. If he withdraws all the money at once, he may lose nearly half to taxes. In the blink of an eye, half a million dollars has dwindled to maybe $200,000 after state and local taxes as well as lawyers and executor's fees are paid. Of course, Robert can opt for an annual distribution to help lessen the sting, but he still must pay taxes on it. The purchase of an EIUL life insurance policy would have circumvented the entire situation, as it allows for tax-free growth, tax-free access by the living, and then a tax-free death benefit.

In another hypothetical, say Mr. and Mrs. Smith are in their early 70s and have no debt. Mr. Smith retired at 66 with a pension, and he and his wife are in good health and draw Social Security. Their son and daughter are both married, with two children apiece. Along with a large savings account of several hundred thousand dollars, the elder Smiths also have $750,000 in several IRAS and don't foresee needing the money at this stage of their lives. But they want control of it, in case anything changes.

Now, the IRS is expecting its cut in the form of a required minimum distribution (RMD), an annual minimum withdrawal from a traditional retirement plan that must be taken by April 1st of the year after the account holder turns 70.5 years of age (and must be taken out by December 31st every year thereafter). The amount of the RMD is based on the fair market value of the plan at the end of the prior year, with the assumed distribution period being based on the life expectancy given the person's current age. This usually means it will increase, although the owner can take out more than the RMD, but never less. And in many cases, the RMD has some unintended consequences, such as throwing the individual(s) into a higher tax bracket (perhaps it's no coincidence that another kind of bomb, the WMD, is only a few letters away on the alphabet).

You are forced to take out money as well as pay higher tax rates on your combined income, which may include Social Security, pension and other forms. In order to circumvent the RMD, the Smiths decided to set up an EIUL policy for themselves (should they ever need it) and their children and grandchildren.

Purchasing the EIUL

In this situation, it may be best to purchase a joint policy; that is, one in which both spouses are the insured. That way, the death benefit pays out when the second person dies. So, if Mr. Smith passes away at age 83, the policy remains in force until Mrs. Smith dies. A joint or combined policy also helps keep down the COI, especially if one spouse is healthier than the other. When properly structured and funded, the EIUL survivor policy will allow for tax-free access to the cash while one or both parties are living, but when they are gone, the tax-free death benefit will help pay off the tax bill for any remaining money still left in traditional retirement accounts.

The first step would be to determine how much cash you want to fund. The Smiths decided to use their RMD, which was $30,000 per year. They still had to pay taxes, of course. In any case, it's best to use underperforming funds; that is, a weaker asset such as a money market account that only earns 1-2 percent. However, you should always keep a "rainy day fund" that can be tapped into without penalties.

After that, follow the standard application procedure discussed in Part 6. Once the policy is approved and issued, you can withdraw the funds from the tax-deferred account and deposit them into a tax-free account. Because it's an EIUL, the rate of return will typically average between 7–9 percent, depending on which company and policy you use.

How it works

The workings of an EIUL can be intricate and complex, which is why it's so important to use a professional with expertise in this area. Let's continue with the example of the Smiths to explain the payout and other benefits.

Because of Mr. And Mrs. Smith's age and health, they were able to get a $1 million survivor EIUL, with a target premium of about $22,000 per year.

Let's say that they both die at age 81. For ten years, from age 71 until death, they deposited $22,000 per year for a total of $220,000 and did not take any cash out of the policy. Once the second spouse passed away, the insurance company delivered a "tax-free" check of $1 million to their heirs.

However, the late Smiths still had the funds from their original IRA, which had been rolled into an equity indexed annuity (EIA), discussed in Part 7. Because EIAs do not have loads, fees or expenses, the Smiths ended up with about the same amount of money that they started with in the IRA, some $750,000. This happened because the indexed annuity offered a "signing bonus" of 10 percent, and they had indexed gains like the life contract. Taxes will be due as funds are taken out by their heirs.

Now the heirs now have the $750,000 that will be taxed and $1 million that is tax free. The heirs can use some of the life insurance proceeds to pay off taxes, pocketing the rest and taking distributions from the IRA when forced to or as needed. Even better, they can invest some of the money from either source and fund their own tax-free future.

Estate Planning Essentials

There are many advantages to estate planning, if only to prevent your heirs from having to go through probate. Probate is the process of the courts determining who gets what and can be very painful and expensive, as well as lengthy and drawn out, as many Americans can attest. It can even involve relatively simple estates if no will is provided.

Life insurance

Life insurance allows you to leverage smaller amounts of money into much larger sums and create an "instant estate." A properly executed policy could take thousands of dollars and create hundreds of thousands or even millions. Yet most people regard life insurance as an unwanted expense that's required to protect loved ones (or as seen on TV shows and in movies, a motive for murder so the villain can collect big bucks). Yet, as previously discussed, life insurance can be used to:

- Create a tax-free retirement account
- Create a tax-free college funding account
- Leverage a small amount of money on children and turn it into large sums of tax-free cash in the future. These monies can be used to fund college, buy a home, start a new business, and eventually, for retirement.

Life insurance and businesses. Business owners can use EIULs to fund retirement while having access to the cash to grow their business or for hard times when "rainy day funds" can be critical.

If they have business partners, they can use what's known as a buy/sell agreement, a contract agreeing to sell part of the business to the surviving partners(s) should one partner pass away. For example, say Bob and James are 50/50 partners in a small construction business. Both are married. They contact a local financial services professional and take out a $1 million EIUL with each other as a beneficiary.

James dies in a car accident five years later and Bob receives the death benefit from the life insurance policy. Per their agreement, Bob pays James' widow the $1 million buyout and now owns the business outright.

Despite the tragedy of James's unexpected and untimely passing, it worked out well for everyone. However, had they not purchased the EIUL, Bob could end up with

James's widow or even grown children as a partner. The business would likely suffer because James was hardworking, experienced, knowledgeable and critical to its success. Since James (and his family) own 50 percent, the survivors' lack of expertise could do great harm to or even destroy the company.

Bob could have even had a buy/sell agreement in place, but without the EIUL to "buy out" James, the agreement is basically worthless. Even if Bob took out a large business loan to buy James' family out, the expenses of paying it off might cripple or possibly destroy the business.

Wills

Every adult should have a least a simple will, a document that instructs how assets are to be transferred upon your death. Templates can come from a number of sources, including the Internet and office supply stores. Wills should be updated on a regular basis and kept in a safe place. A simple will should be sufficient if you have an average amount of assets. If you are married, then the spouse will, unless otherwise instructed, inherit any assets you leave behind.

If you get divorced, make sure to update your last will and testament or your ex-spouse might end up with money and other assets intended for children, the new spouse or others. Sitting down with a lawyer and paying a modest fee to put together a will is a small investment and will protect a lifetime worth of assets. Otherwise, the courts, probate and lawyers may also end up with much of that hard earned money.

Trusts

You'll need a trust if you have a large number of qualified and non-qualified assets, real estate and business interests. Nonqualified assets include cash, such as money in a checking or savings account or in a safe, or funds in a money market. Taxes have been paid on these monies and no future income taxes will be due. Qualified monies are funds in an IRA, 401(k,) 403(b), 457 fund or a thrift savings plan. No taxes have been paid so it will be all taxed at current tax rates for the owner at the time of distribution.

Consult an estate attorney specializing in trust work to help you position assets to minimize the tax burden to your heirs. Again, you'll need to periodically revisit the trust because tax laws change; for example, private letter rulings from the IRS can affect ongoing strategies.

Both trusts and "living wills" can also be used to provide directives to loved ones regarding your wishes concerning end of life decisions.

Summary

A small inheritance will probably have little or no effect on your income tax bill, but a larger sum could force you into a higher tax bracket each year you take a distribution and/or payout. Proper financial planning with help ensure that Uncle Sam won't end up with money that was supposed to be yours.

Summary: Some Final Answers

Questions and Answers

Although much of this information was covered in previous chapters, below are some commonly asked questions and answers relating to EIULs and indexed life insurance.

What's the difference between permanent life insurance and an annuity?

Permanent life insurance is a contract between the insured/policy owner and a life insurance company. The insured has to pass a medical exam, and a death benefit is part of the contact. The insured pays a premium, whether monthly, quarterly, semi-annually or annually. With an EIUL, a portion of the premium goes to cover the cost of insurance (COI) or death benefit, with the remainder going in an accumulation account that tracks a stock index, such as the S&P 500, NASDAQ or Dow Jones.

Each policy has a minimum premium and maximum amounts. The minimum is set by the insurance company, and the maximum is set by the IRS. Each policy also has a maximum annual amount or modified endowment contract (MEC) guideline, which is solely based on IRS regulations regarding age, sex, health and death benefits. As long as you don't deposit more than the maximum or MEC guideline limits, the funds can be accessed income tax free while living, and the remaining funds pass to the beneficiaries, also income tax free. The applicable MEC guidelines, IRS Code 7702 and 72e, have allowed for tax-free accumulation, tax-free living access and for the remaining amounts to be passed to heirs income tax free. Depending on the life insurance policy, tax-free funds can also be accessed for college, emergencies, retirement or any other purpose, regardless of age.

Annuities are savings vehicles typically offered by insurance companies. Non-qualified money, or cash, deposited into these accounts grows taxed deferred, but the owner would pay taxes on just the gains, not the original principal. Money withdrawn before age 59 ½ is subject to a 10 percent penalty from the IRS, much like an IRA. Unlike an IRA however, the owner of a non-qualified annuity is not required to take a required minimum distribution (RMD), an annual minimum withdrawal at age 70½.

Many Americans are rolling 401(k)s, IRAs, TSPs, SEP IRAs and all types of qualified money into an annuity. Done properly, it's a rollover, or trustee-to-trustee transfer, meaning that the annuity becomes an IRA. All IRA rules apply to the annuity, regardless of owner. Money withdrawn before age 59½ is subject to a 10 percent early withdraw penalty, and since income taxes have never been paid, they will now be due. RMDs at age 70½ still apply because it's an IRA, and beneficiaries will also have to pay taxes when they withdraw funds once they take ownership of the accounts.

Are life insurance distributions taxed? What happens when I die?

The way to get money out of a permanent life insurance contract tax-free is to withdraw the principle and borrow the gains. For example, say you live to be 100 and have taken $1 million out of a $5 million dollar policy. Upon your death, the insurance company pays themselves back out of your account and sends whatever's left to your family or heirs, who receive it tax-free.

Each policy has guidelines and/or provisions dictating the rate of interest you may borrow at and what rate of return your money will earn during the duration of the loan. As described earlier, wash or zero cost loans make it very attractive to access monies from these policies. When a policy-holder requests a loan from their account, the insurance company lends it out of the company's cash reserves. The cash value in the policy-holder's account is used as collateral.

For example, if you borrow $100,000 from your policy, the insurance company would take money from their cash reserves and send you a check. Since it's a loan and not income, no taxes are due. If the insurance company charges you 6 percent for the loan, however, your $100,000 is still sitting in your account earning 6 percent, therefore making it a wash or zero cost to access your funds.

How does this money shake out with income tax reporting?

If you are taking the money out of the policy, it's a loan and therefore not taxable income. If your heirs are receiving it as part of an insurance settlement, it's not taxable either. This is true, regardless of the amount involved.

Can Congress or the IRS change the tax laws in the future?

They have tried a number of times over the years. However, laws are already in place that "grandfather" existing policies; that is, any changes would only apply to new policies issued after the date the new law was passed. So, if you purchase a policy before the law was changed, you are protected and won't be penalized.

With the government needing so much money these days, won't it take away the tax exemption of life insurance?

Probably not, for several reasons:

- People tend to be shortsighted and focus on the short-term cost and not the tax-free windfall they will receive later. Legislators realize this.

- Our government is broke. This is why they encourage tax-deductible charitable contributions;

the more we give, the lesser burden it puts on Uncle Sam. It's the same with life insurance, which helps take care of our families so they don't have to.

- 80 percent of senators and representatives use the life insurance exemption themselves. Why would legislators wipe out a perk that benefits them?

In the case of a Roth IRA, clients who purchase a life insurance contract agree to pay taxes now on the funds being deposited, so the government gets paid now. The trillions of dollars in IRAs are taxed later, meaning that the government has agreed to wait until a date in the future. I would be more worried about changes to those tax laws.

How difficult is it to pass the medical exam?

That depends upon the individual insurance company; some companies are more conservative than others. However, many options are available if you have health issues. Modern medicine can solve some problems, or if your spouse is healthy, you can take out a policy on him/her. If both husband and wife are ill, a policy may be taken out on a child, even an adult, if there is an insurable interest. This means that your life would be damaged financially if that child were to pass away. The object here is to fund an account for wealth creation. You own the policy and the cash that funds it, and therefore you control it.

Can I use the EIUL to fund my child's college?

Yes. Not only can you pull from life insurance to pay college expenses tax-free, but investing income in life insurance may also lower your tax reporting income, helping your children qualify for grants, scholarships and other types of student aid. Even very wealthy people use insurance policies as a tax shelter.

Do insurance companies charge to take out a loan on your policy?

Of course; they need to make money too and will charge you interest. However, depending upon the policy, you may have a couple of options, which basically cost you nothing and might even earn a little. You can take out a "wash" or zero cost loan, which charges X percent or the exact percentage the money is earning in the account anyway. Even better, though is a variable loan. Say you still pay 6 percent interest for a $70,000 loan, but it's in a contract earning 8.81 percent, so you are actually making money when you borrow. How cool is that?

What if somebody had a beneficiary IRA? Would it make sense to roll it into an EIUL?

I would suggest rolling this type of money into an indexed annuity, which would become an IRA. That will help avoid incurring losses or penalties.

If the life insurance premiums go up as you get older,
how do the terms on your life insurance plan change?

In the past, most people wanted the most life insurance for as little money as possible. Here's five cents, give me a $10 million policy. However, properly designed EIULs are vastly different; you want maximum cash going into the policy with the smallest death benefit allowed by IRS regulations. That way, your cash has the ability to grow, with only a small portion of your payment going to the death benefit itself.

A life insurance professional will help you find a policy that, as you age, can be filled with cash and minimizes the cost of insurance. As you withdraw funds, the policy death benefit drops dollar for dollar. This minimizes costs, maximizes returns and keeps the IRS happy.

What if I need the money unexpectedly?

Depending on the policy and how it's funded, most EIUL-type life insurance policies have exceptional liquidity after just a few years, which allow you to access cash quickly. In the past, it might have been years before you could get to any of the cash value. Of course, this depended on the contract and how you were funding it.

With EIULs, if you are "max" funding it or depositing large sums of cash, then you typically have a greater percentage of accessible cash, in many cases within 12–24 months of starting and funding the policy. For example, one of my clients had deposited $100,000 in a policy over the course of about a year and was faced with an unexpected and dire business emergency. This was in 2008, and the U.S.

banks were in a panic and very tight-fisted with loans. Even though he was worth over $4 million on paper, his bank still turned him down, despite the fact that they'd done business together for several decades.

However, with his signature on a form, and after a few business days passed, he was able to borrow $70,000 against his EIUL policy and therefore save his business. And it doesn't have to be an emergency; some people borrow to start a company, buy a car or for college funding. However, remember that if you take out a loan like this, you should repay it as soon as possible if your goal is a tax-free retirement.

Are there any downsides to depositing money in a life insurance policy?

Rather than being considered as a traditional investment, an EIUL has a death benefit of life insurance and an accumulation account that is "linked" to a stock market index. This is how it differs so drastically from other types of insurance policies.

The only downside would be failure to deposit the scheduled amount of funds without lowering the death benefit. For example, say Joe planned on depositing $10,000 per year for 15 years into a $500,000 EIUL. After eight years, he can't, or chooses not to, deposit the funds for the next seven years. Joe should request that the insurance company lower the death benefit to perhaps $300,000. Doing this maximizes the $80,000 already deposited. If he leaves the original death benefit in place, too much of his cash will pay for the death benefit and not enough will be put in the accumulation account. However, please be aware of the strict IRS guidelines on lowering the death benefit, and consult a life insurance professional and the insurance company before making any changes.

How many years does it typically take to fund a policy?

The fastest you can fund a policy is three years and one day (four years) if you are under 50 years old, and four years and one day (five years) if you are over 50. Payments can be made monthly, quarterly, semi-annually or annually. Many options are available, but the faster you get the money into the account, the quicker the compounding effect works.

What are the fees?

Fees vary according to product and company policies. The basic costs are a sales charge, COI, and administrative fees. A sales charge may be between 5-7.5 percent and is a one-time charge of funds being deposited into the policy. While it may seem like a hefty fee (for example, 5 percent of an $80,000 total deposit is $4,000), it is far lower than a 20-50 percent future income tax rate. Administrative fees average about $10 per month, depending upon the company. The COI is based on age, sex of insured, health and the size of the policy.

How can I be sure that the insurance company won't go belly up? Is there any recourse, government or otherwise, that can protect me from unscrupulous insurance companies?

Make sure they are part of the Legal Reserve System, which requires that participating companies hold strong cash reserves in order to meet all their policy obligations. These reserves are based on actuarial formulas and are designed to allow the company to meet all of its financial obligations. Each state also has an insurance commissioner who oversees companies statewide and reviews performance, making sure companies meet all requirements.

Also, working with a reputable and experienced insurance professional will help you find the most stable company and lucrative policy.

What funds can be put into the EIUL?

Any underperforming funds can be used, from cash to money market accounts to savings to money originally slated for a 401(k), IRA, TSP or any retirement account. Some people have refinanced a home, consolidated debt and then used that money to fund the account.

Is there a limit on who can fund an EIUL and how much money can be deposited?

Anyone, regardless of age or income, can fund an EIUL. You can put anything from a few thousand to millions of dollars into these accounts. People fund EIULs primarily for the consistent rate of return and the tax-free living access to the cash.

Can children fund an EIUL?

Yes, although as with any insurance policy, health status comes into play. Most insurance companies allow these types of policies to be taken out on children of all ages, although there are different rules as to how much insurance a child can have. Most companies also require that the parents have a policy in place. Small amounts of money funded over just a few years can create large sums of tax-free cash for the future.

Can someone in their 70s or older fund an EIUL?

Yes, although every situation is different. Younger people may use the EIUL for both wealth creation and the need for the death benefit to protect loved ones. Those in their 70s and older may use these types of products for estate planning, but in many cases their goals and needs are different. They want a decent rate of return and like the benefit of income tax-free living access to their money and income tax-free transfer to their heirs.

I have an old permanent life insurance policy. Can I move my cash value into these newer products?

Yes, although you must still pass the medical exam. In most cases, a transaction known as a 1035 exchange will allow movement of cash from one policy to another. Improved rates of return, cost of insurance that has been discounted over the years, liquidity and loan provisions make this an attractive decision.

Can I move my 401(k) or IRA into an equity index policy?

If you are over 59 ½ years old, you can move money from a qualified plan into an equity index life contract. Depending on your needs, desires and assets, this could be an effective way to go from tax-deferred to tax-free. Check with your CPA; everyone involved in the plan should agree that it is in your best interest. If you are under 59 ½, however, there are early withdrawal penalties, so you might want to wait until you reach this age.

About the Author

Steve Burton is the founder and president of Equity 1 Inc. Financial Solutions. Along with protecting and growing money through unique programs, Equity 1 helps people find "lost funds" to enhance their portfolios. A radio talk show host for many years, Steve has also come to be known for his no-nonsense, common sense approach to money. His weekly features on the economics of politics find him "ranting" on the irrational mismanagement of our nation's funds by those in elected office.

Steve has also given hundreds of seminars that introduce proven strategies using 21st century "hybrid" products to make money in both good times and bad. These workshops have taught people of all ages that, unless they are properly funded, mortgages and other so-called "secure" investments can actually destroy, rather than create, wealth.

Born in Ohio and raised in Virginia by a police captain father and a stay-at-home mom, Steve learned and maintained a strong work ethic from an early age. He was employed by the Secret Service for three years while attending school, but his love of business won over his interest in police work.

Steve has started and purchased many enterprises over the years, but the desire to help others create wealth finally led him to the financial services business in the 1990s. The thrill of helping people to improve their lives in the short term while at the same time creating and achieving long term financial freedom motivates him. Many have asked Steve why he works so hard, and his response is that this is as much fun for him as playing golf or shopping.

Steve has been married to his wife Annette for over 30 years and they have two sons, Kevin and Adam. They currently reside in Virginia.

Retirement Money Wave

The Seven Retirement Money Wave Rules

Rule 1: Save more

Rule 2: Live on at least 15 percent less than you earn

Rule 3: Practice discipline in putting money away
for retirement

Rule 4: Manage your debt

Rule 5: Know the difference between good and bad debt

Rule 6: Reduce your tax liabilities – tax deferred is
not tax free

Rule 7: Put your money in life insurance and other
secure investments